Celtic Knots

Adult Coloring Book

Lorraine Kelly

Lozs Art

lozsart.com

Twitter @lozsloot

Facebook LozsArt

DeviantArt - LorraineKelly

tumblr.com/blog/lozs-art

Test your pencils & pens:

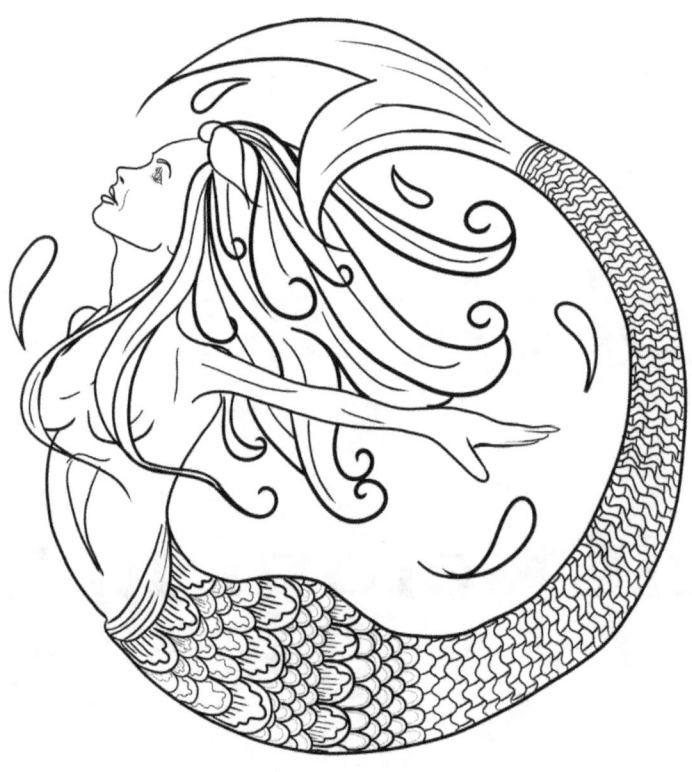

Like LozsArt on facebook to share your colored pictures and to keep up to date with new books and offers.

Please respect the copyright of images within this book and only share your colored pages.

About The Artwork

Some of the traditional designs in this book have been inspired from The Book of Kells, which is a beautifully illuminated manuscript Gospel book. It is believed to have been created c800 and is regarded as an Irish national treasure.

The author also gained inspiration and instruction on knot-work from George Bain's classic book: "Celtic Art, the Methods of Construction", first published in 1951

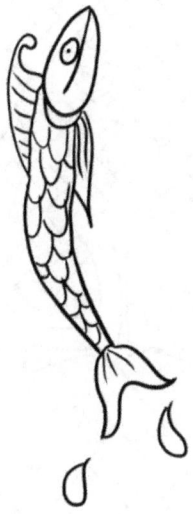

About Lorraine Kelly

Lorraine Kelly is a self-taught artist. Originally she worked in the finance industry in Perth, Western Australia. After marrying. she had a sea-change and moved to the South-West of Western Australia to raise their family. During this time, she began her own business on eBay selling her hand-painted glassware and craft items. This is her first coloring book, but she has been selling her own artwork and prints on Etsy and eBay.

Deluxe editions with thick, quality paper, or digital downloads for self-printing are available on these sites.

lozsart.com

stores.ebay.com.au/Lozs-Loot

www.etsy.com/au/shop/LozsArt

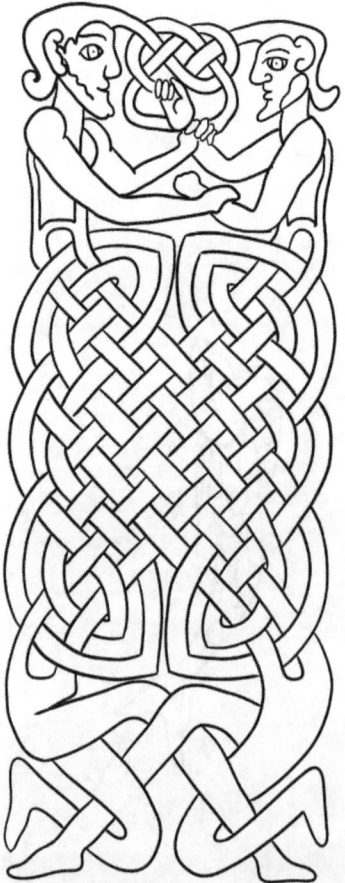

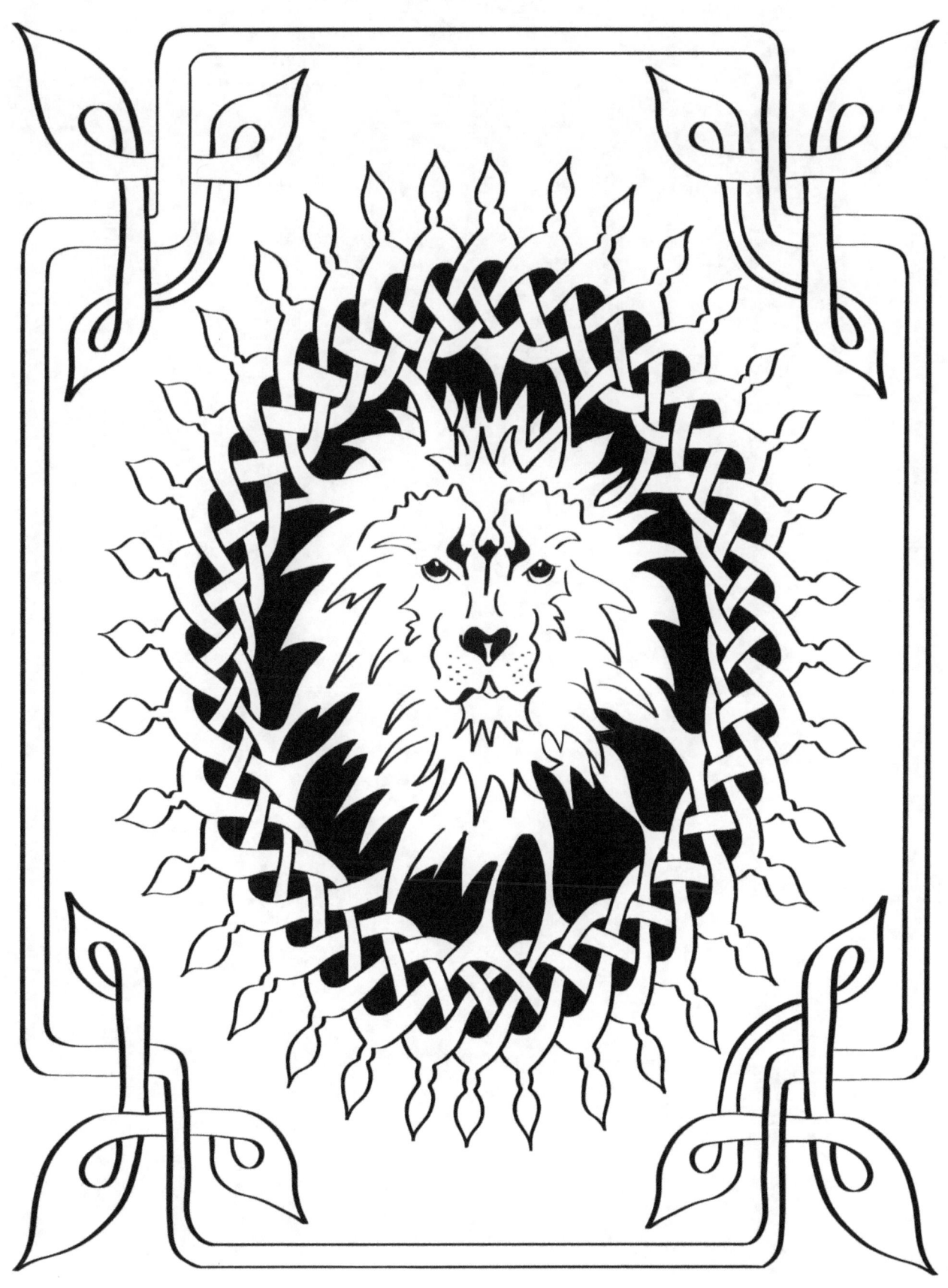

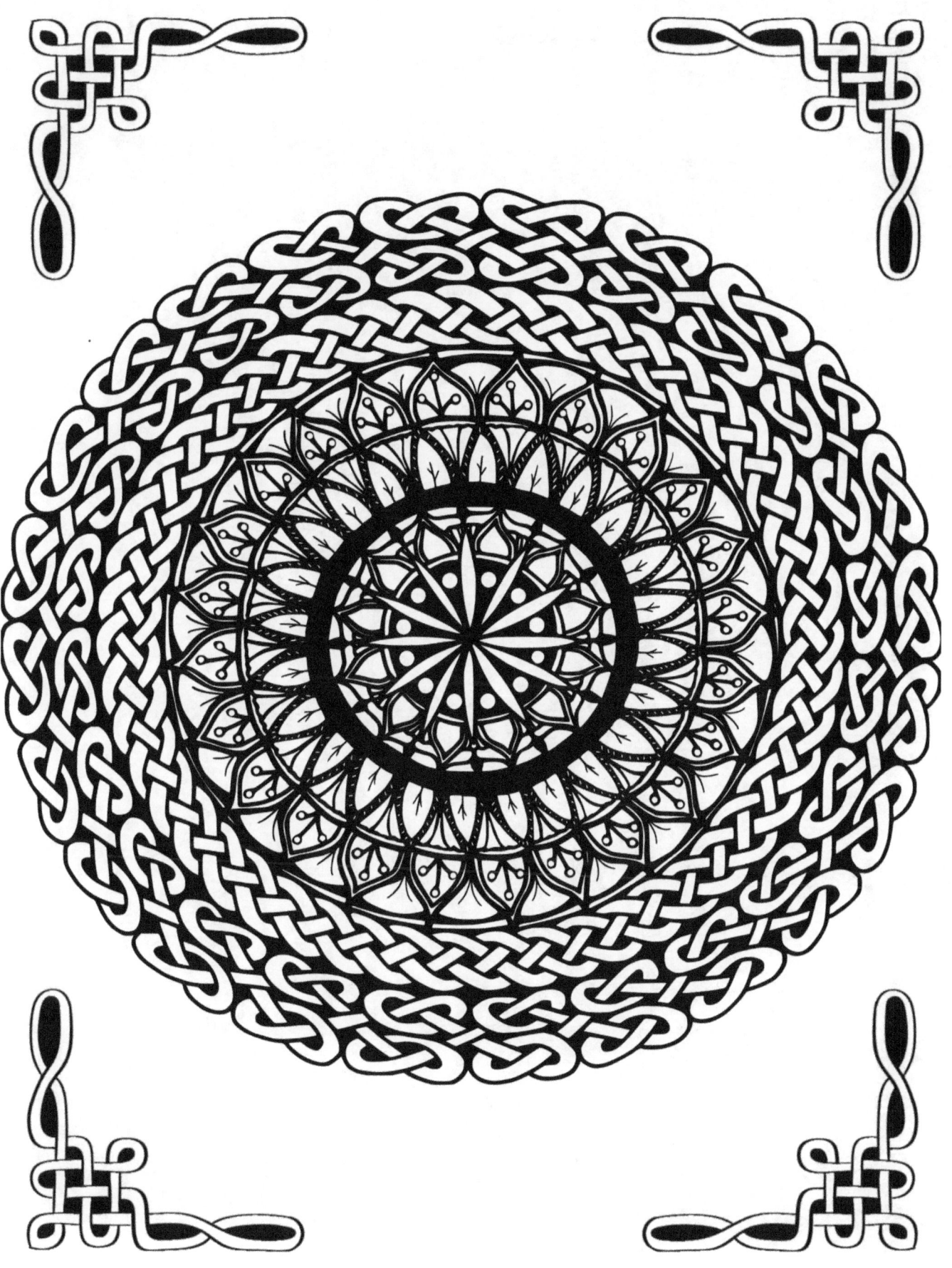

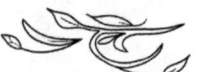

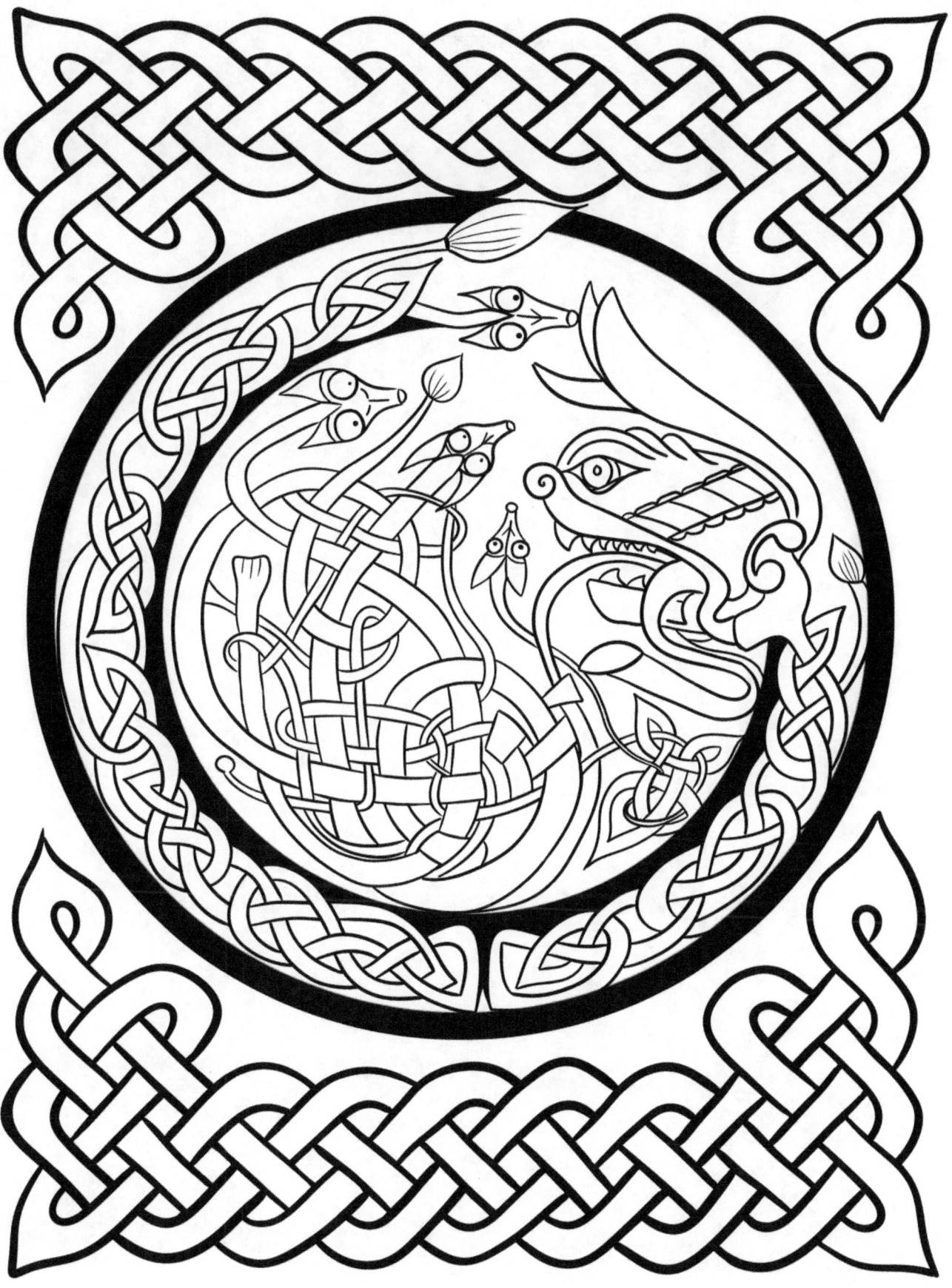

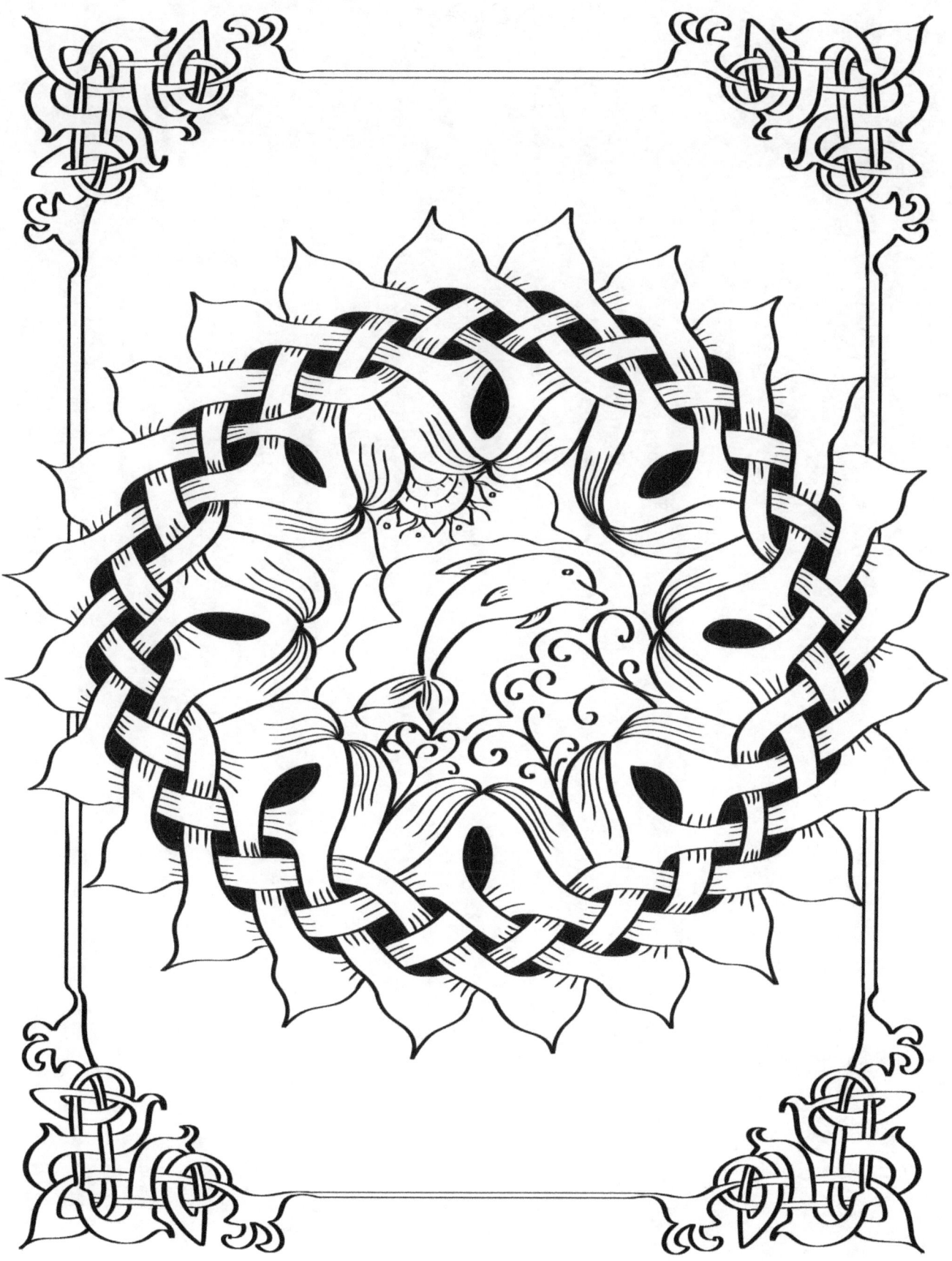

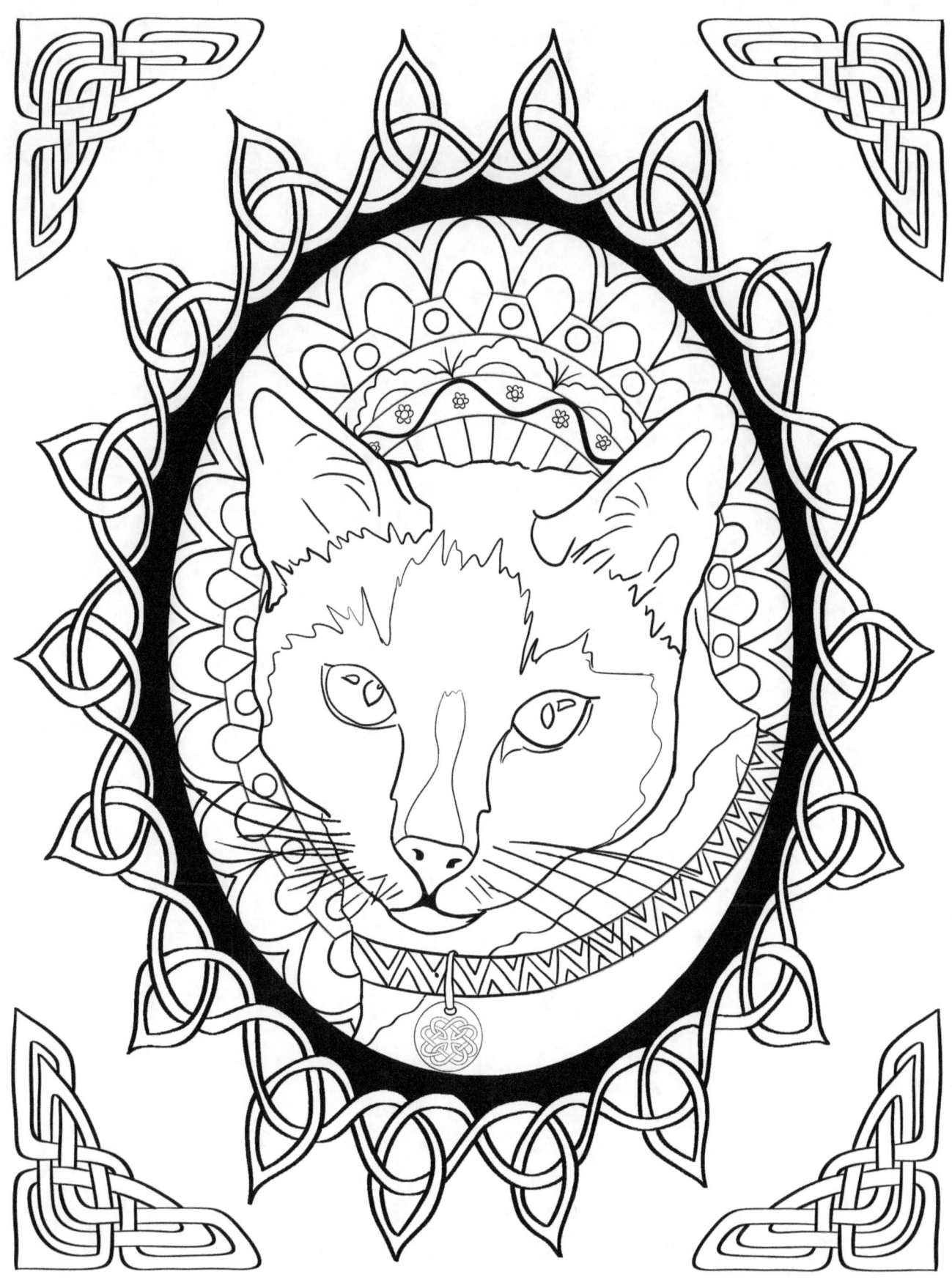

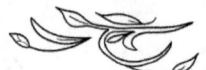

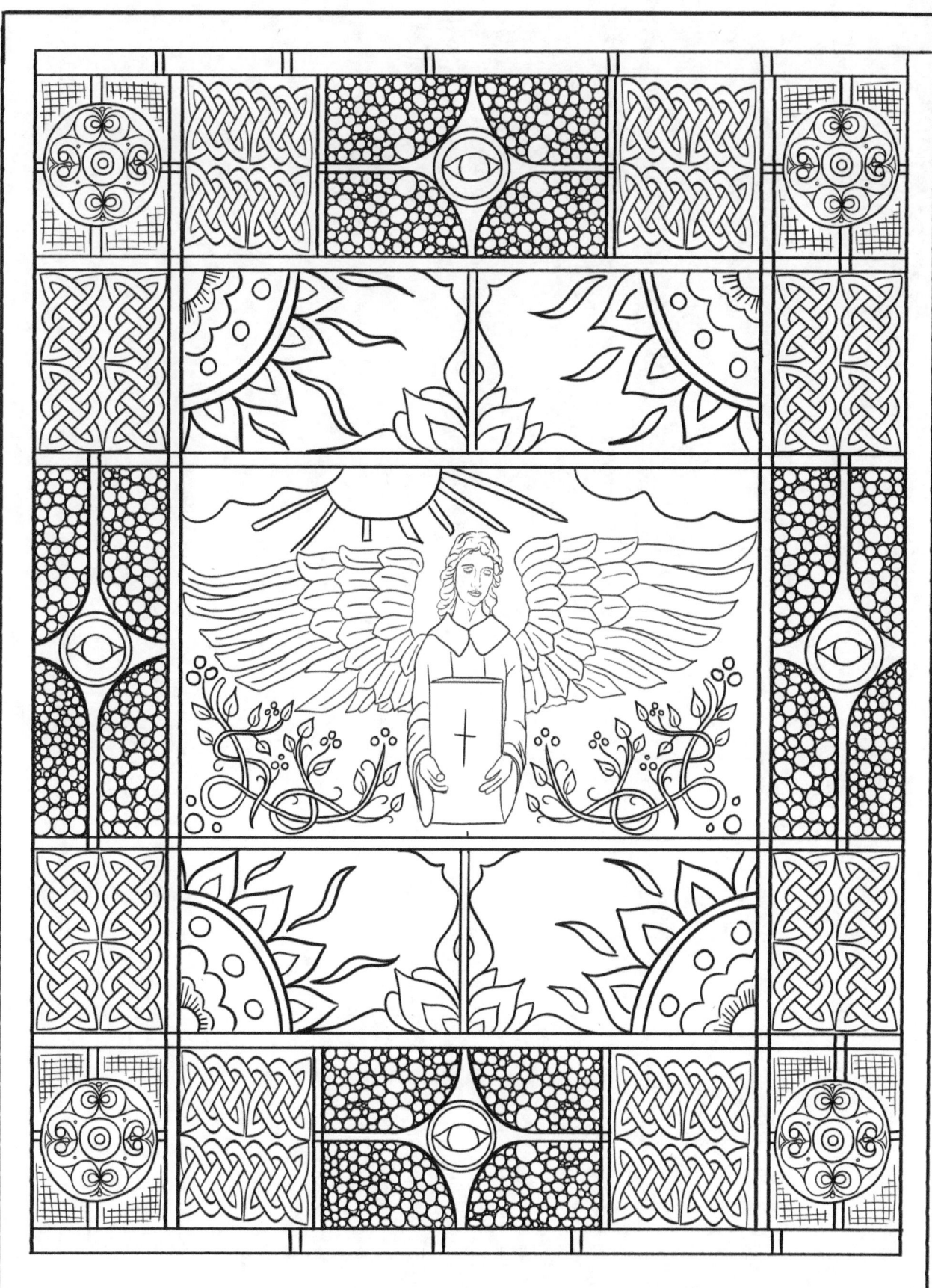

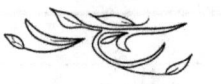

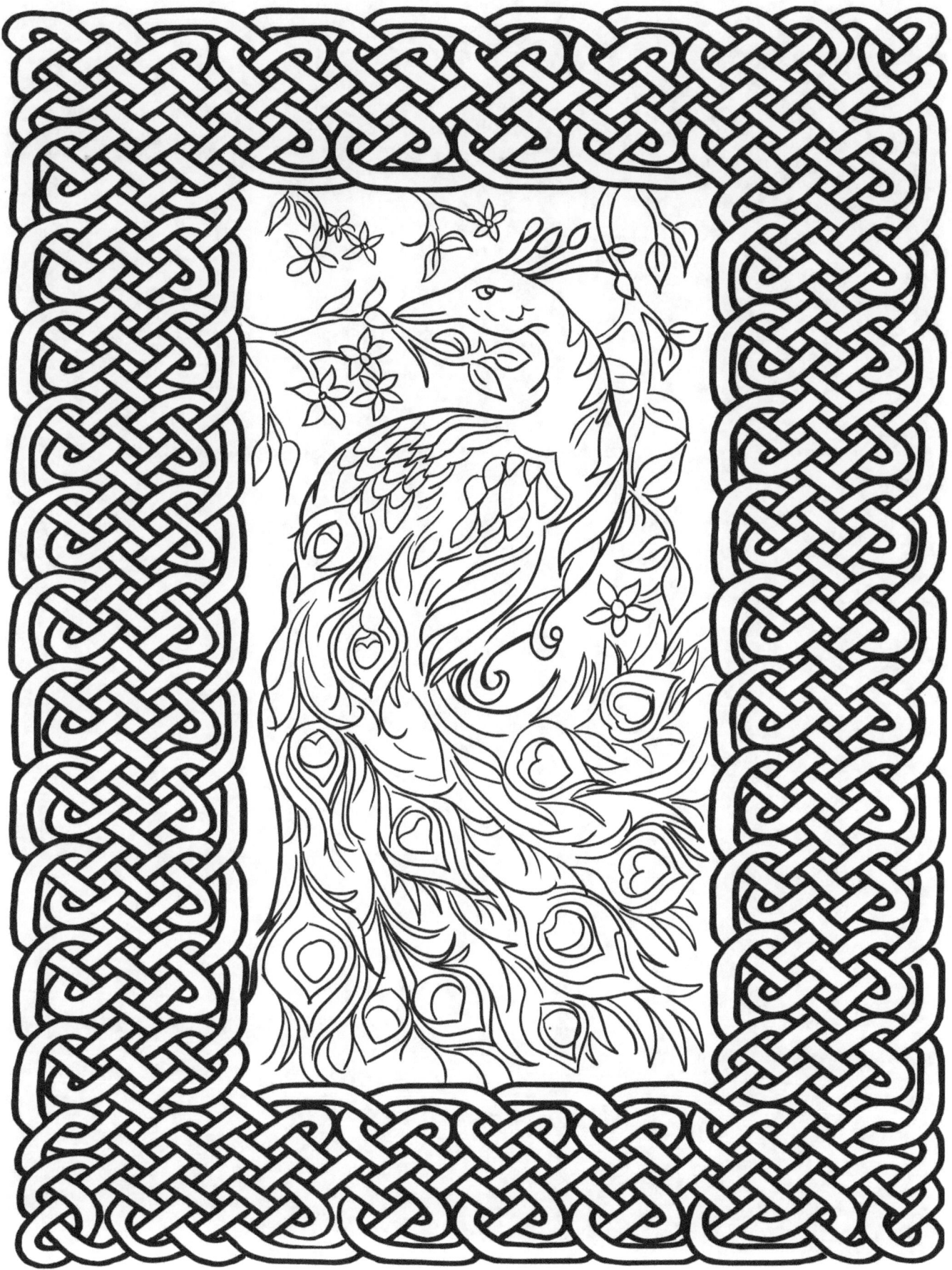

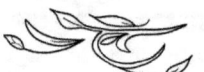

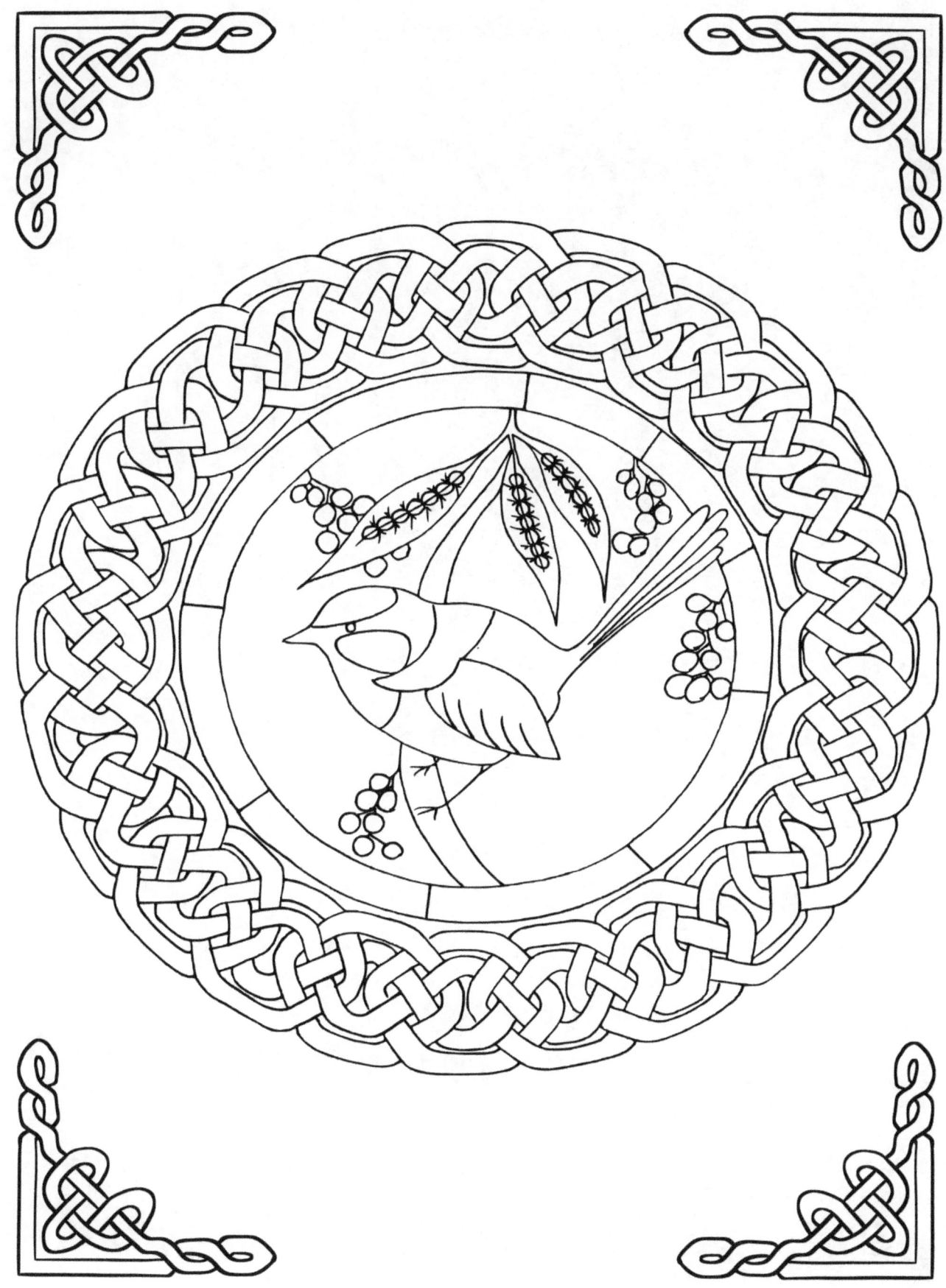

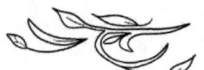

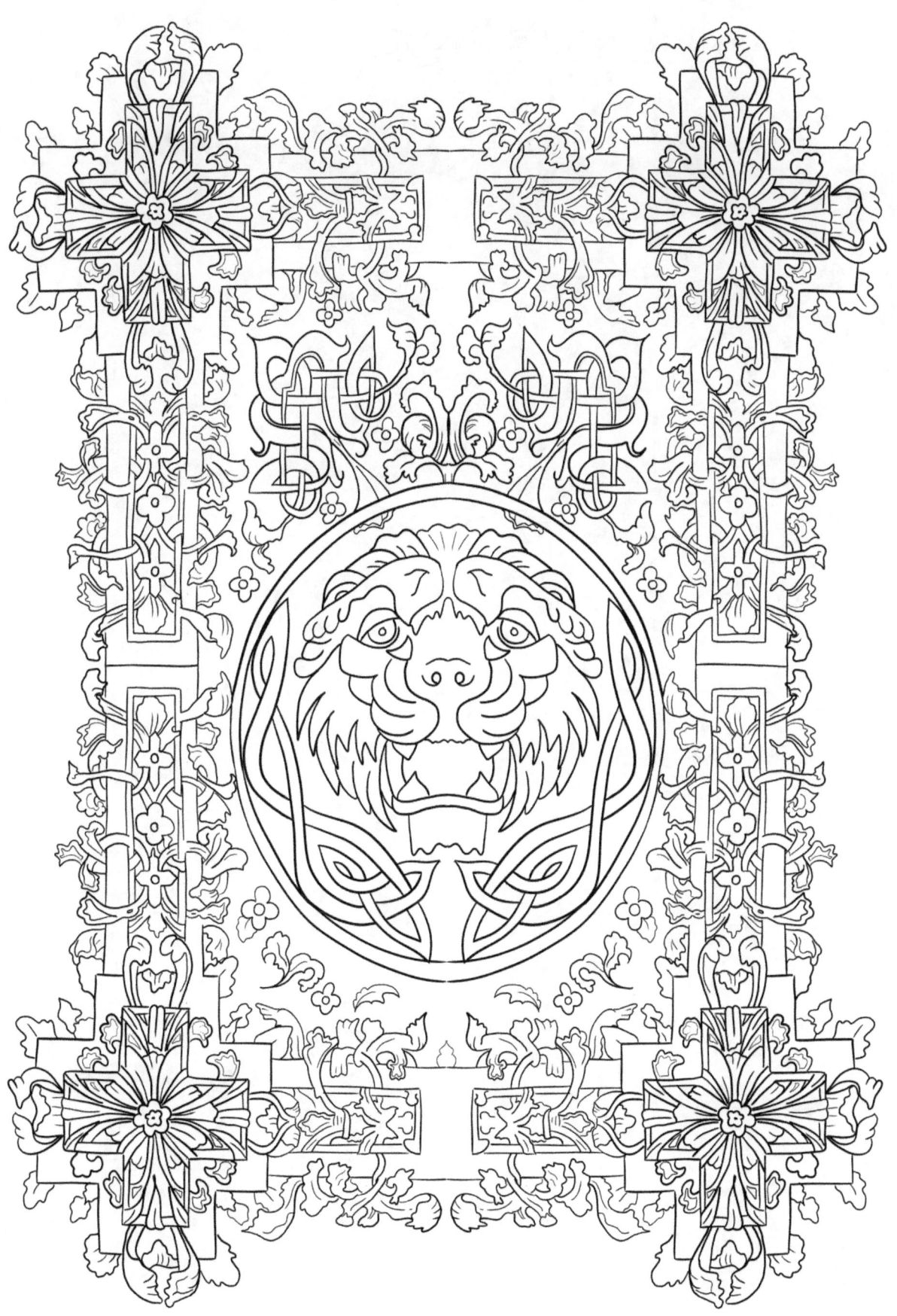

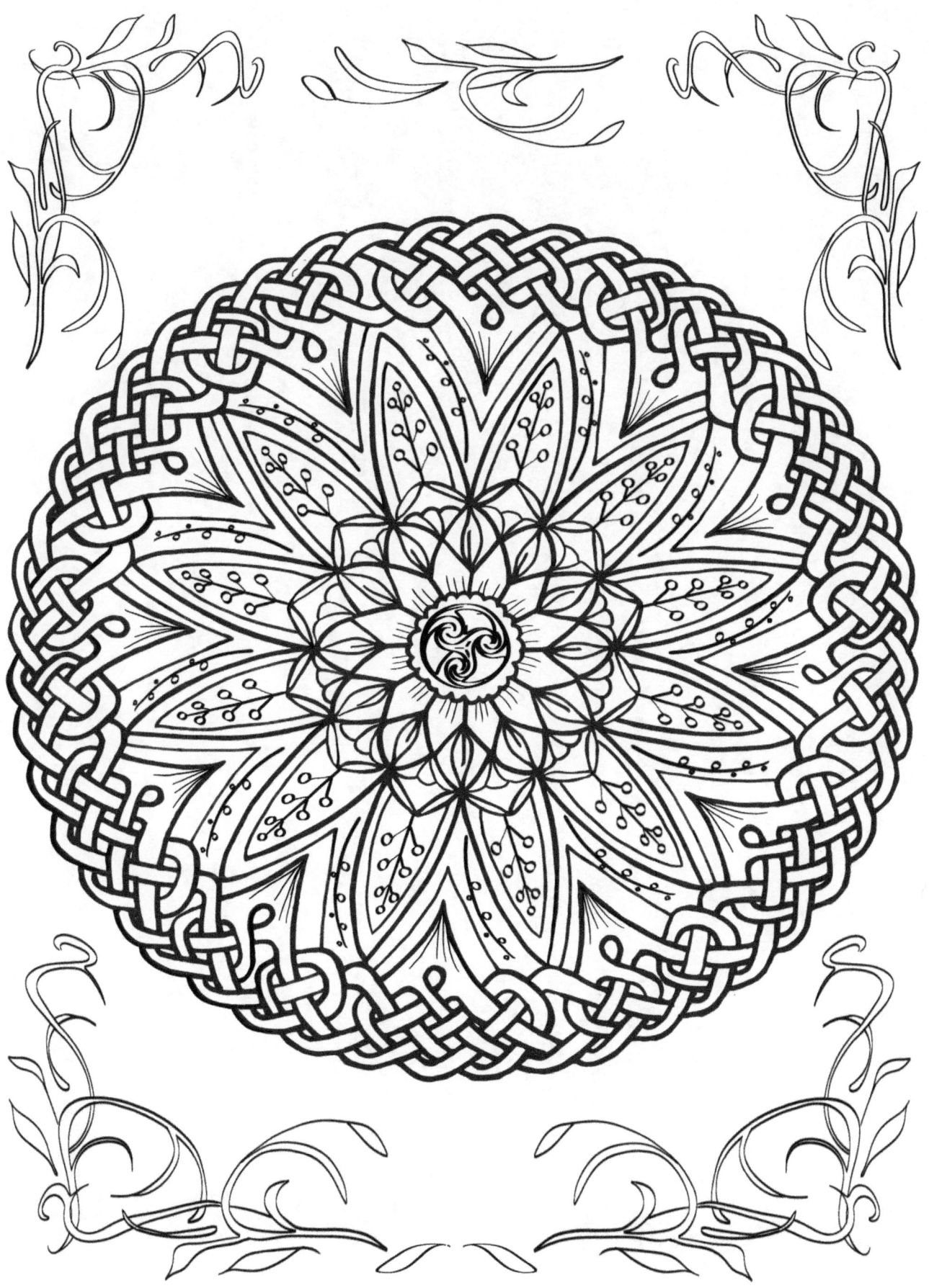

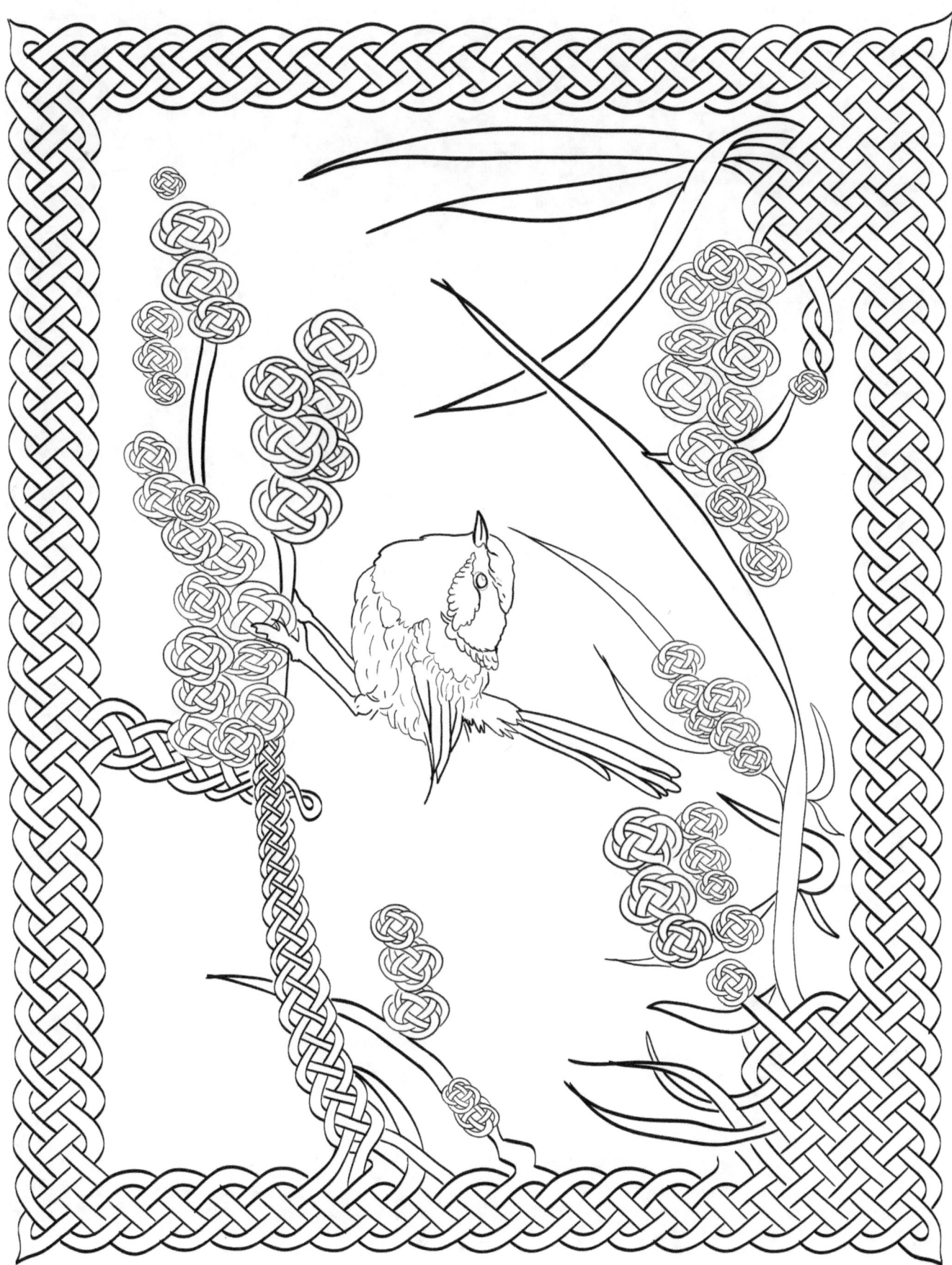

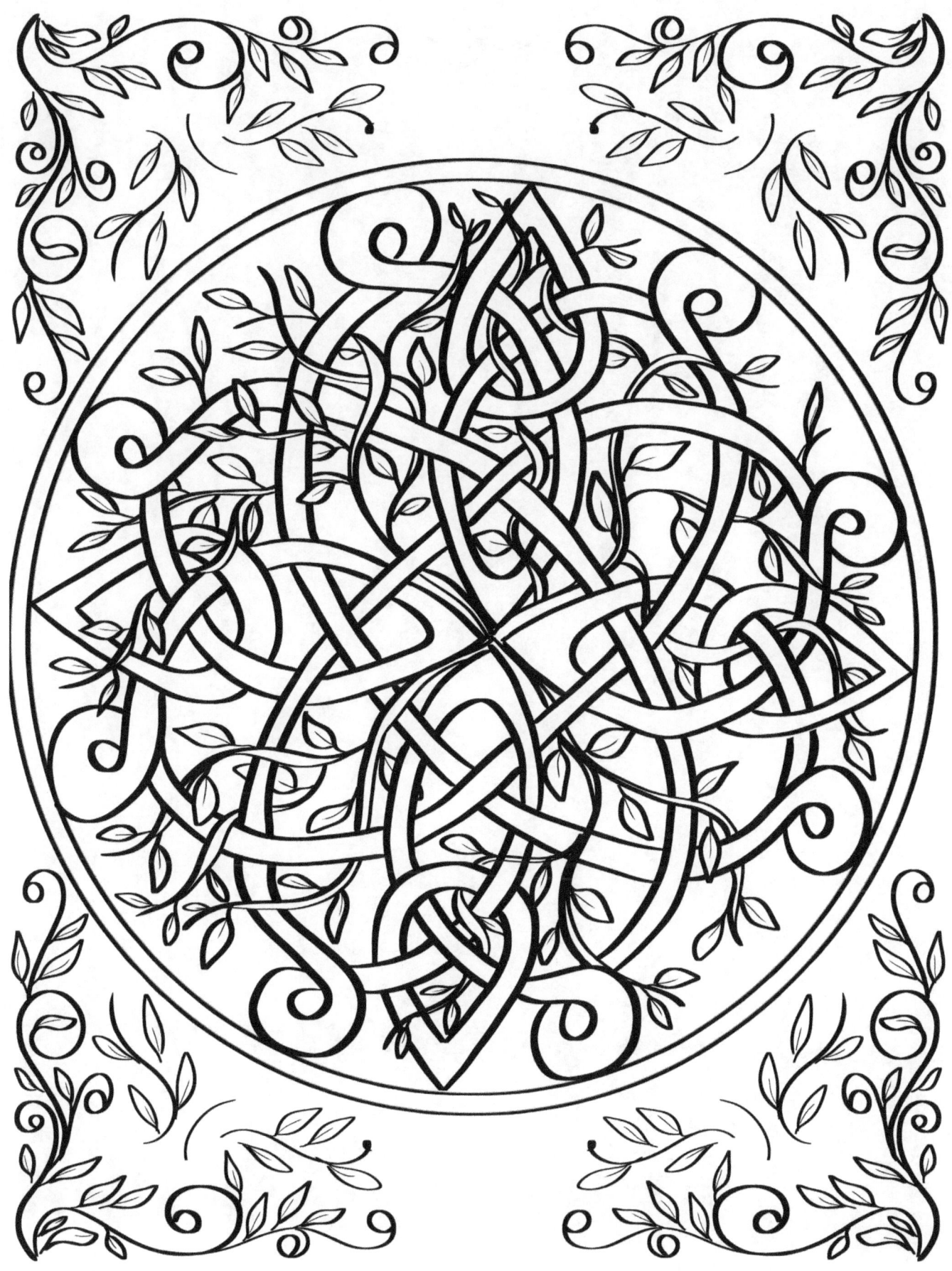

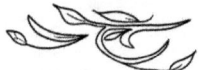

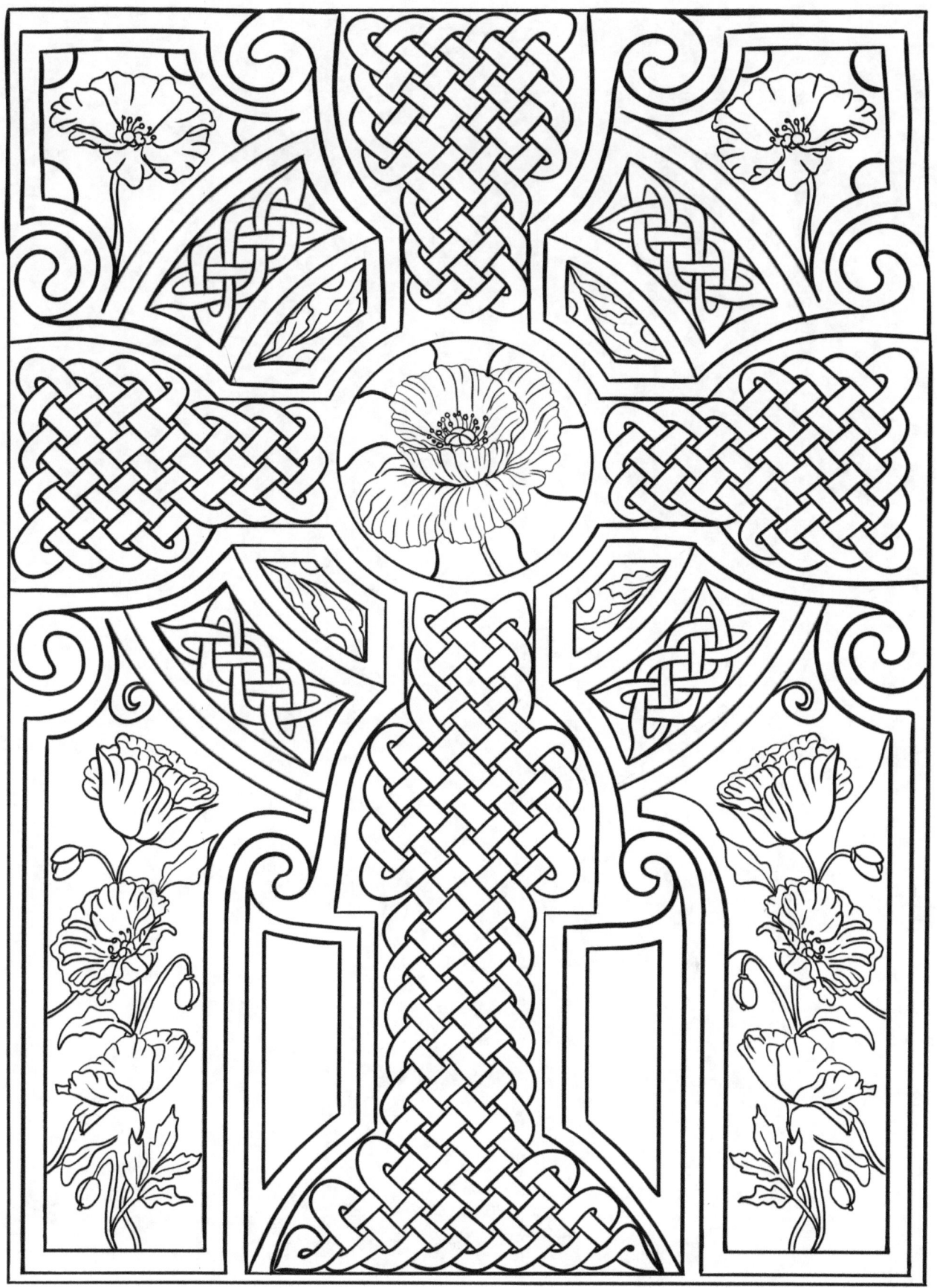

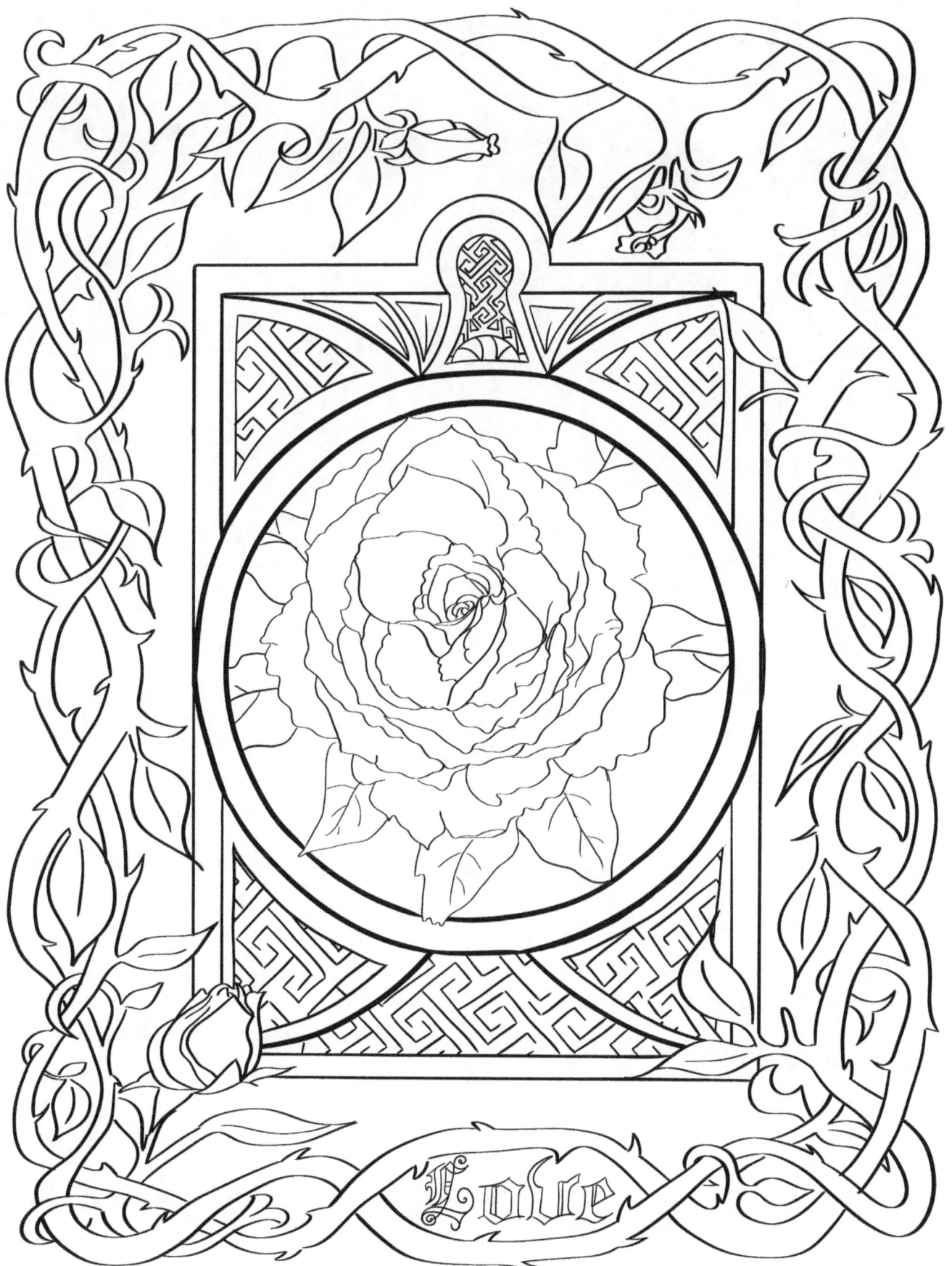

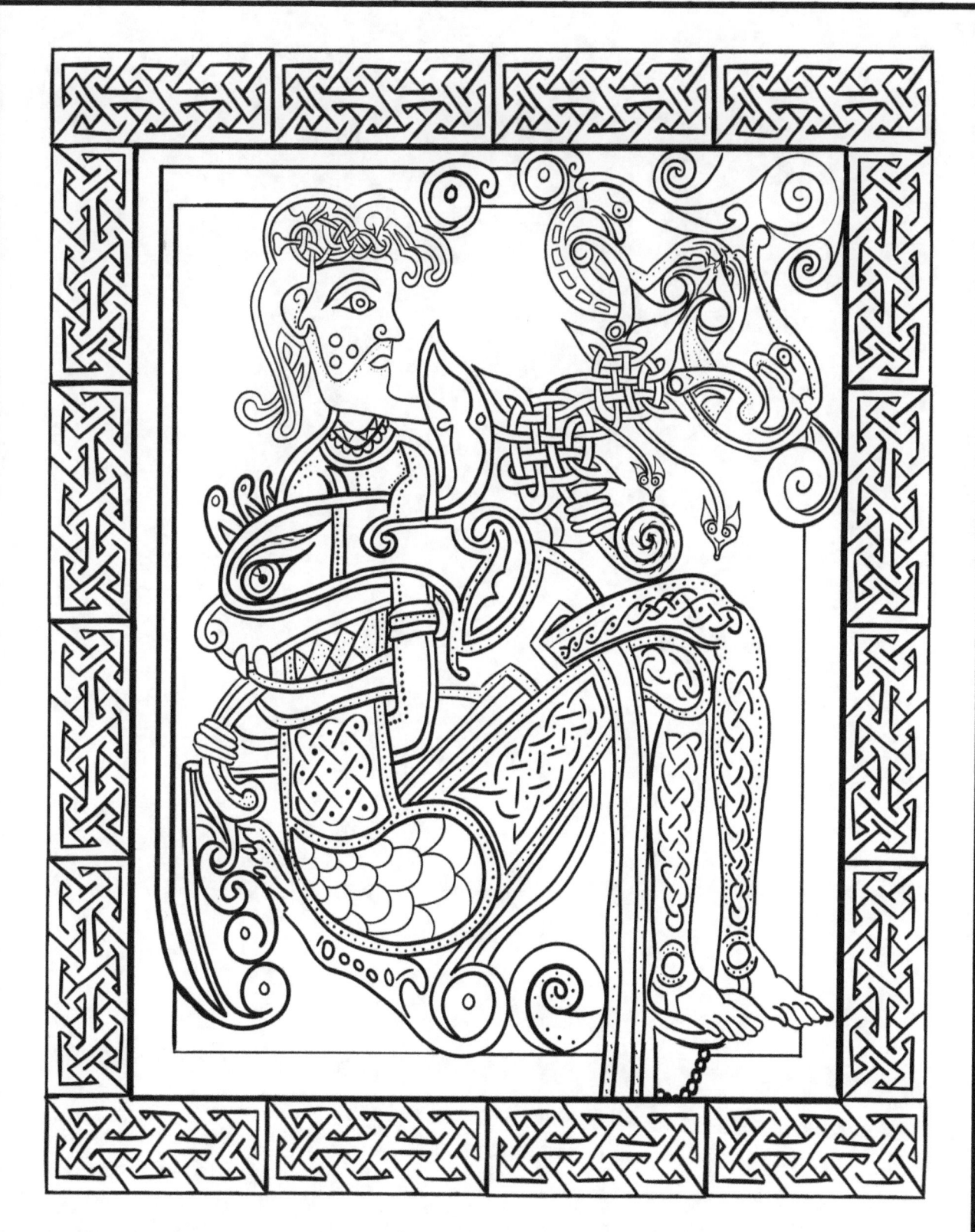

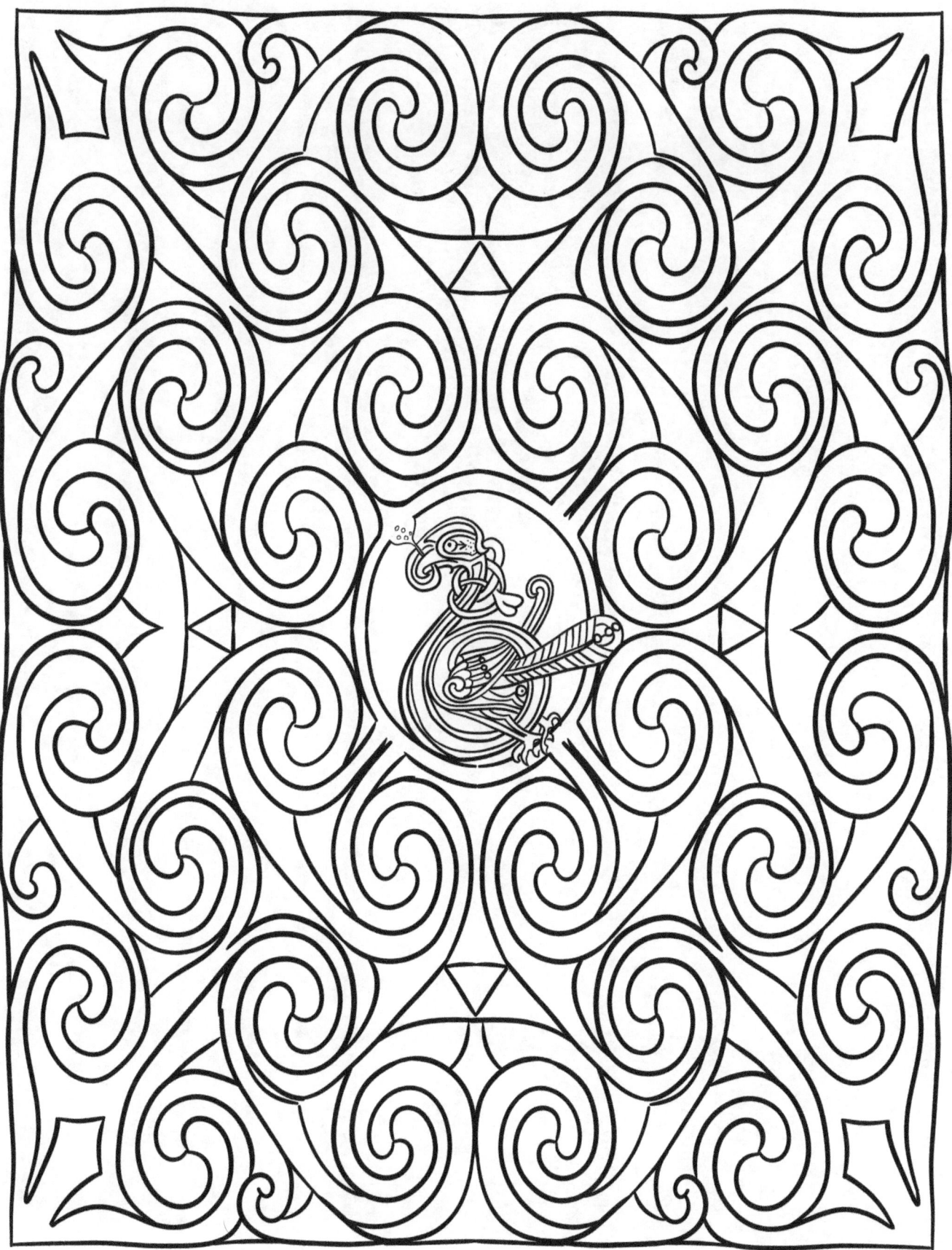

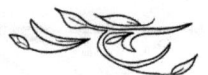

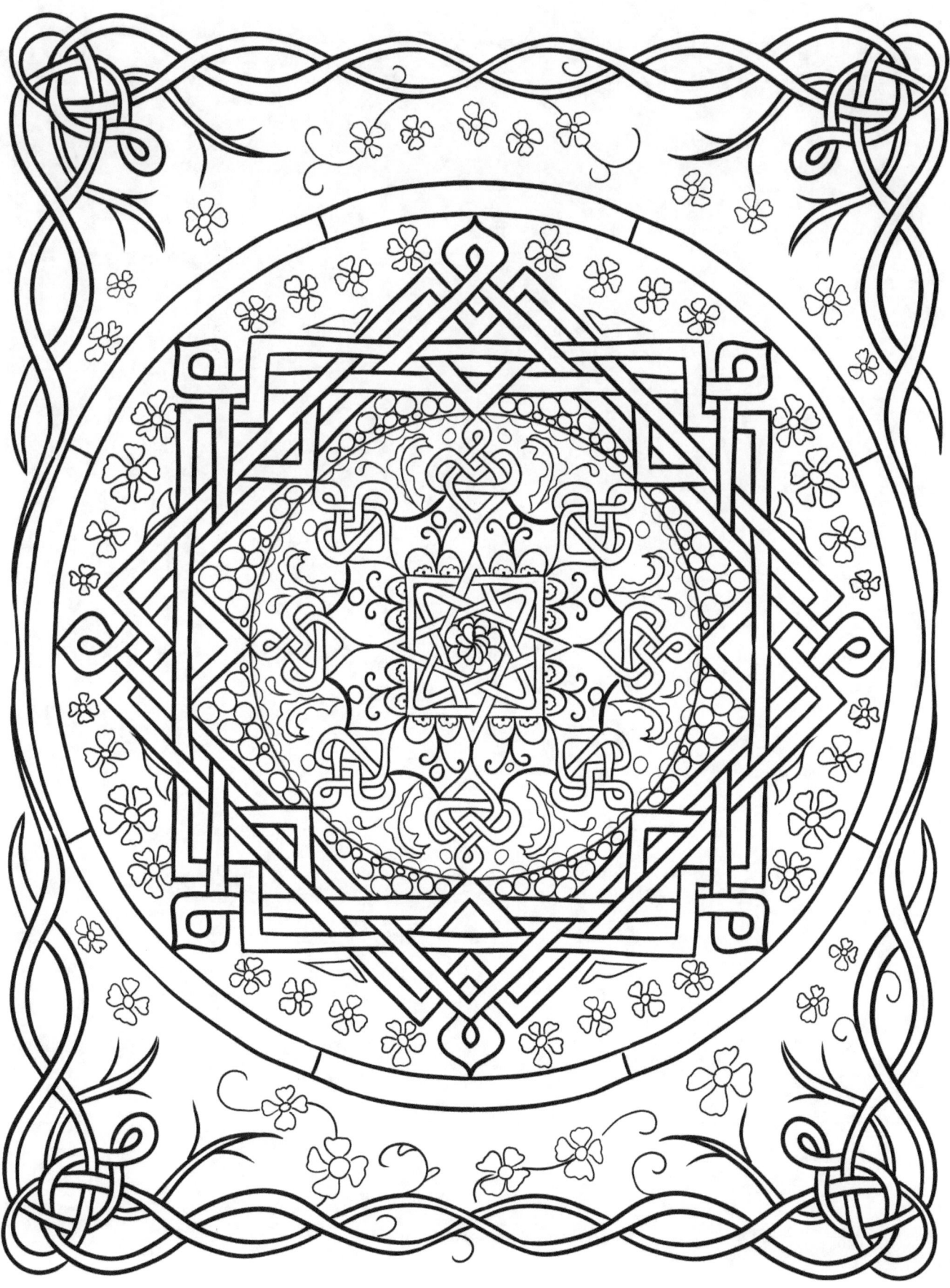

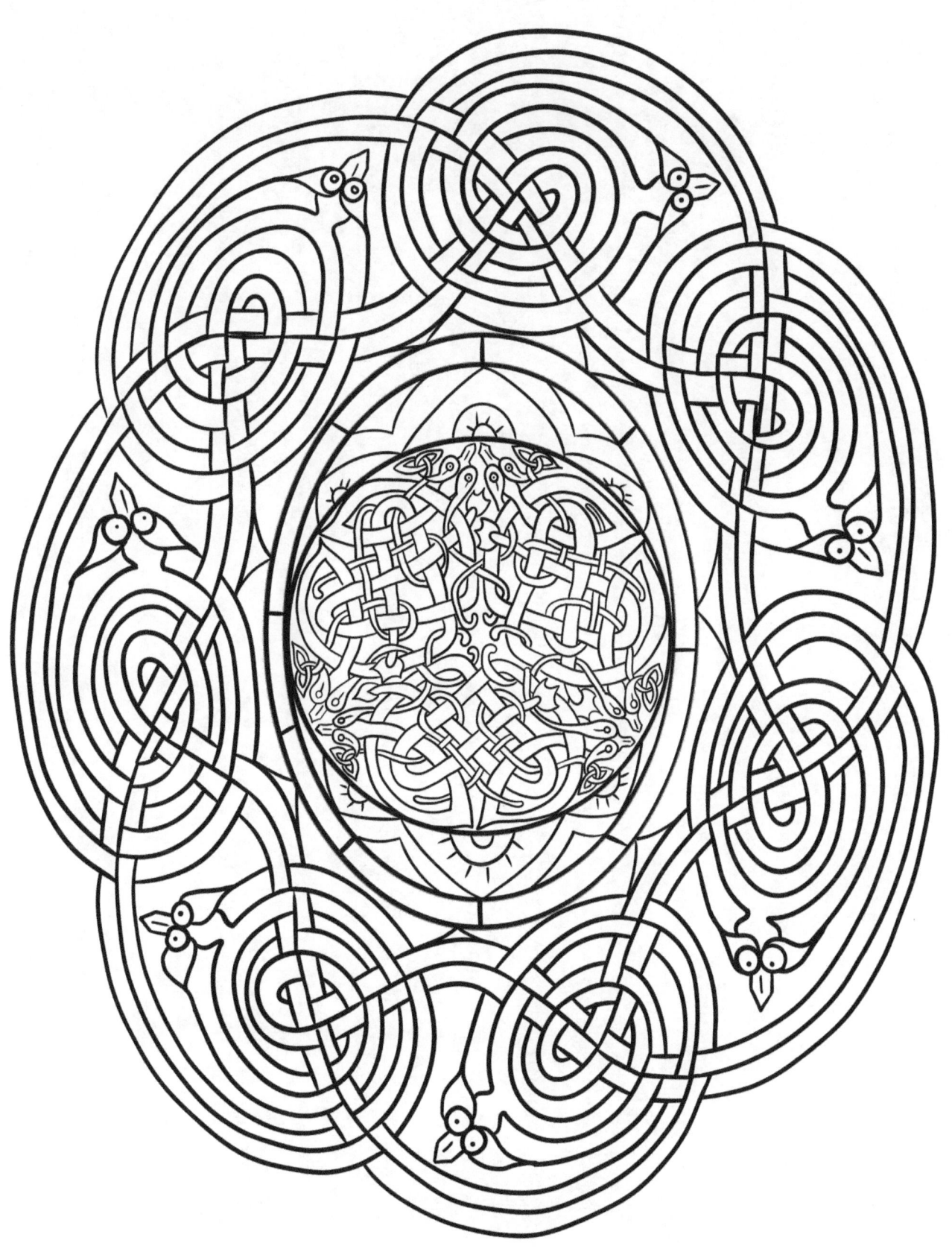

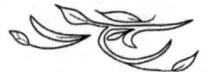

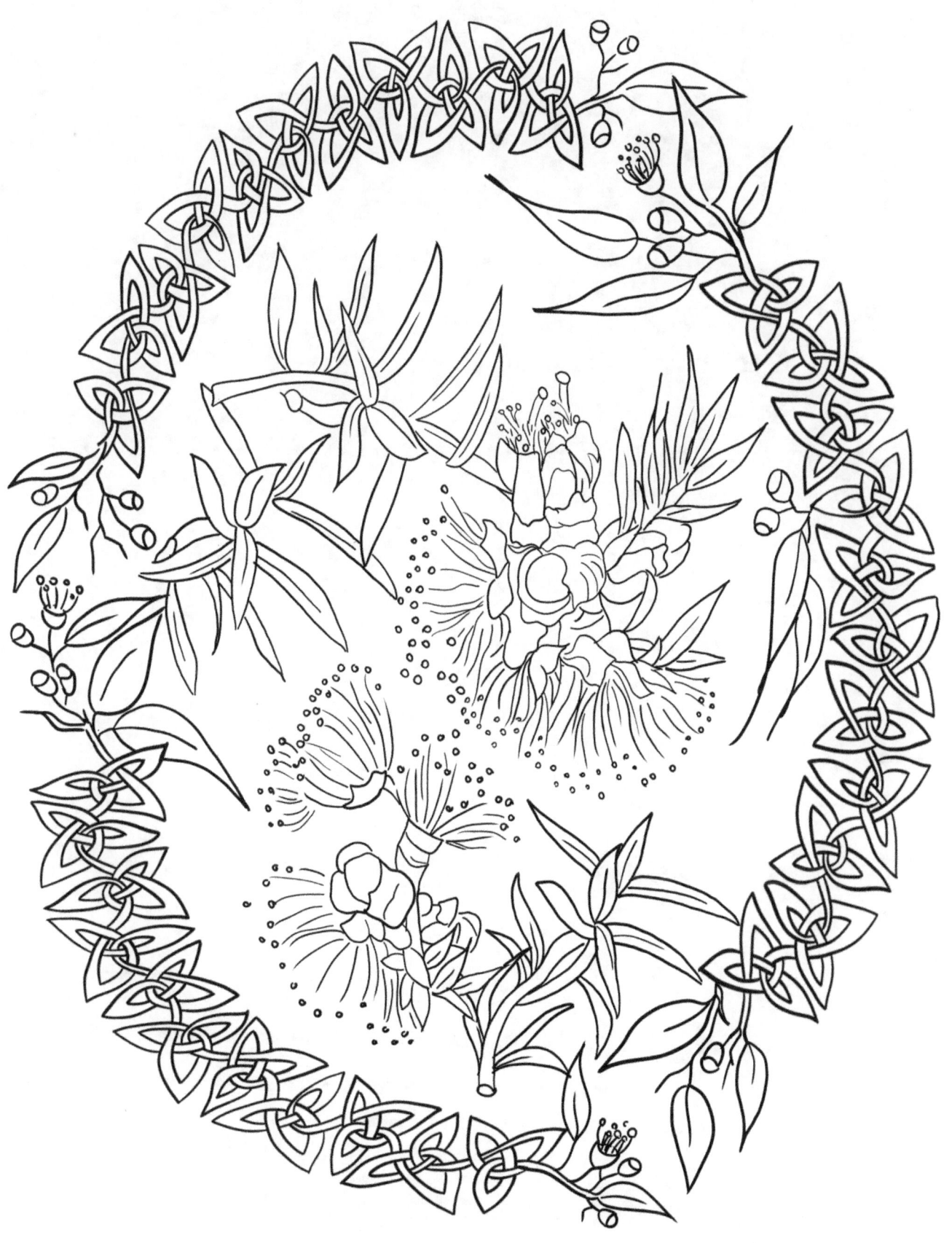

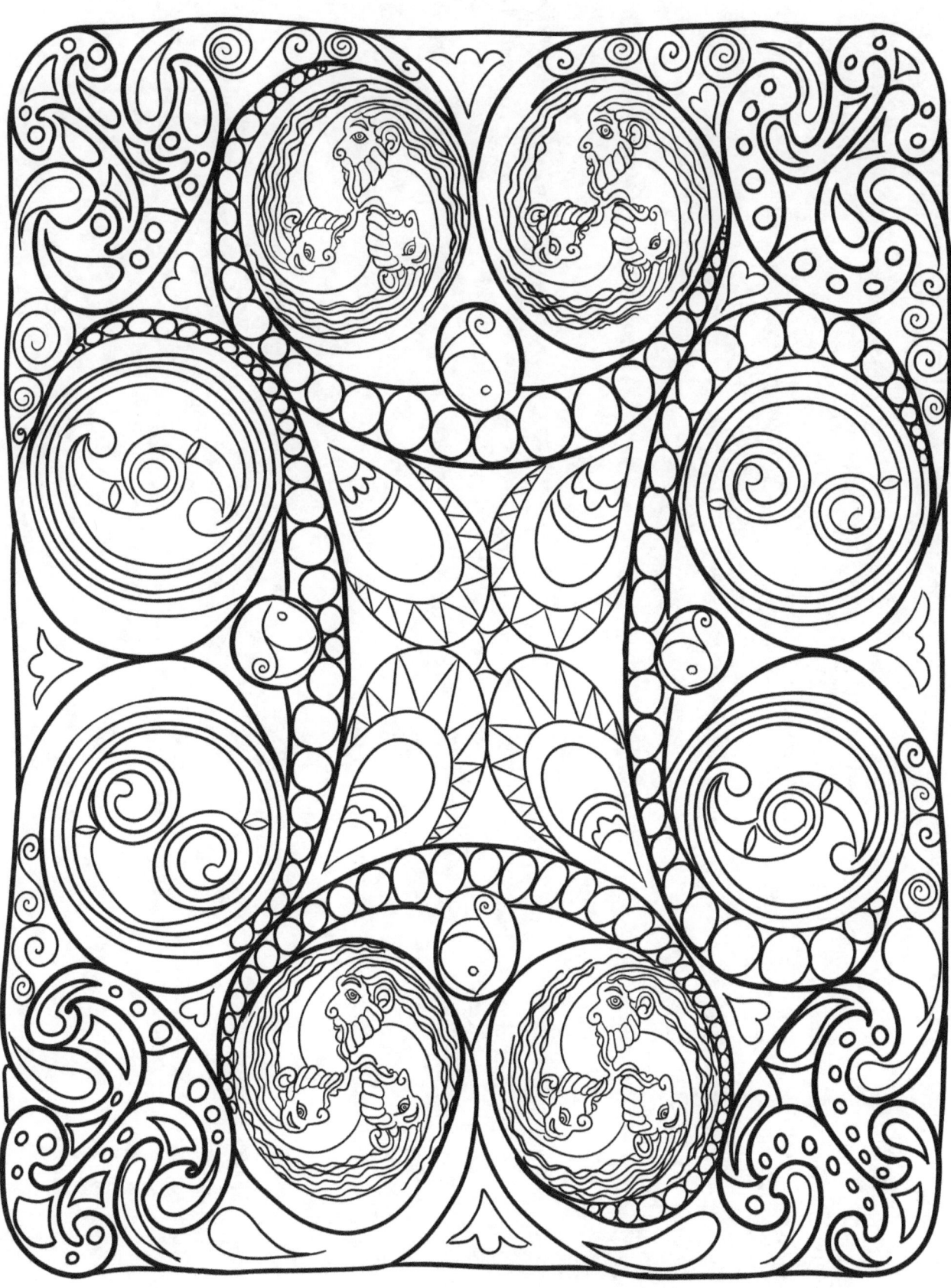

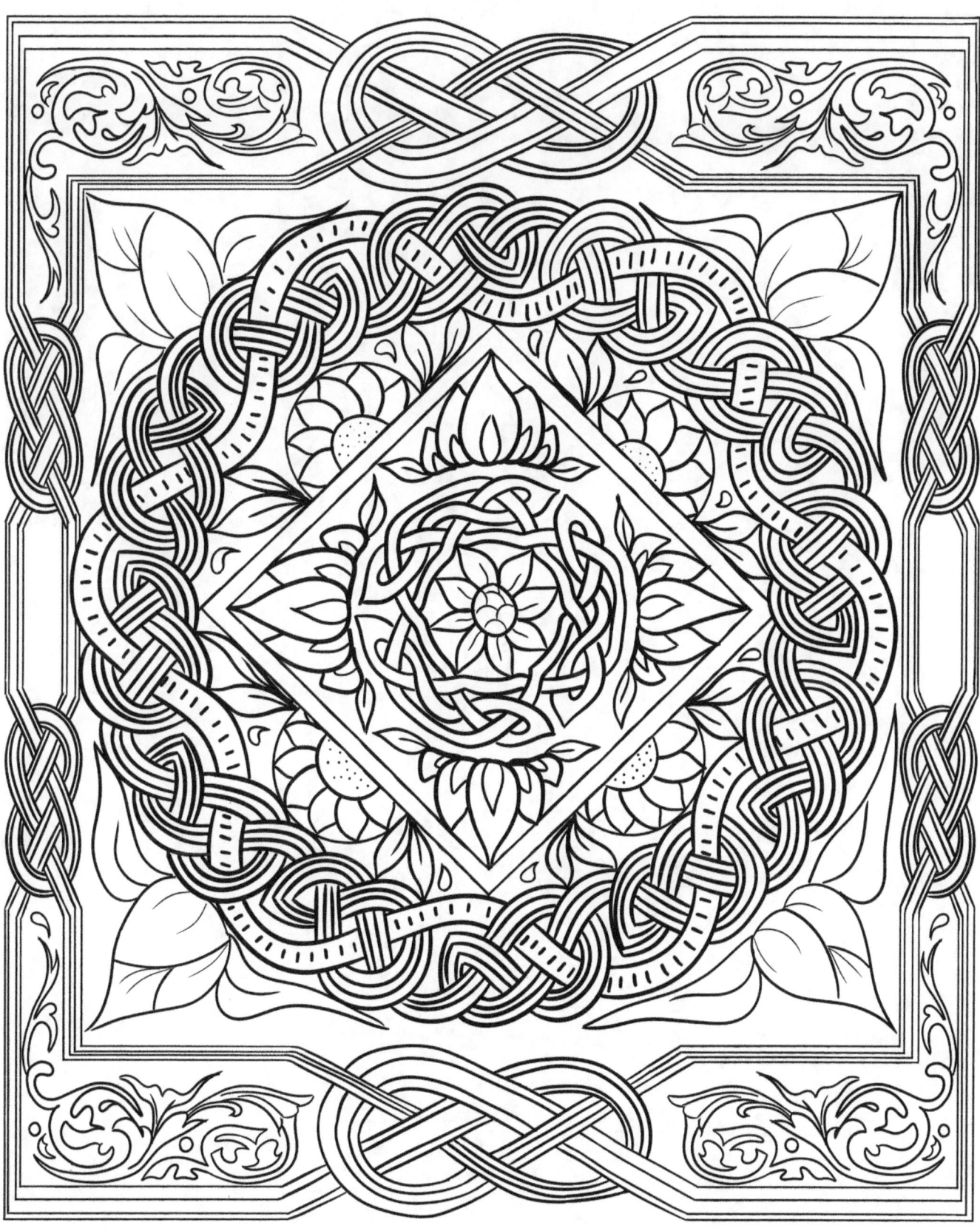

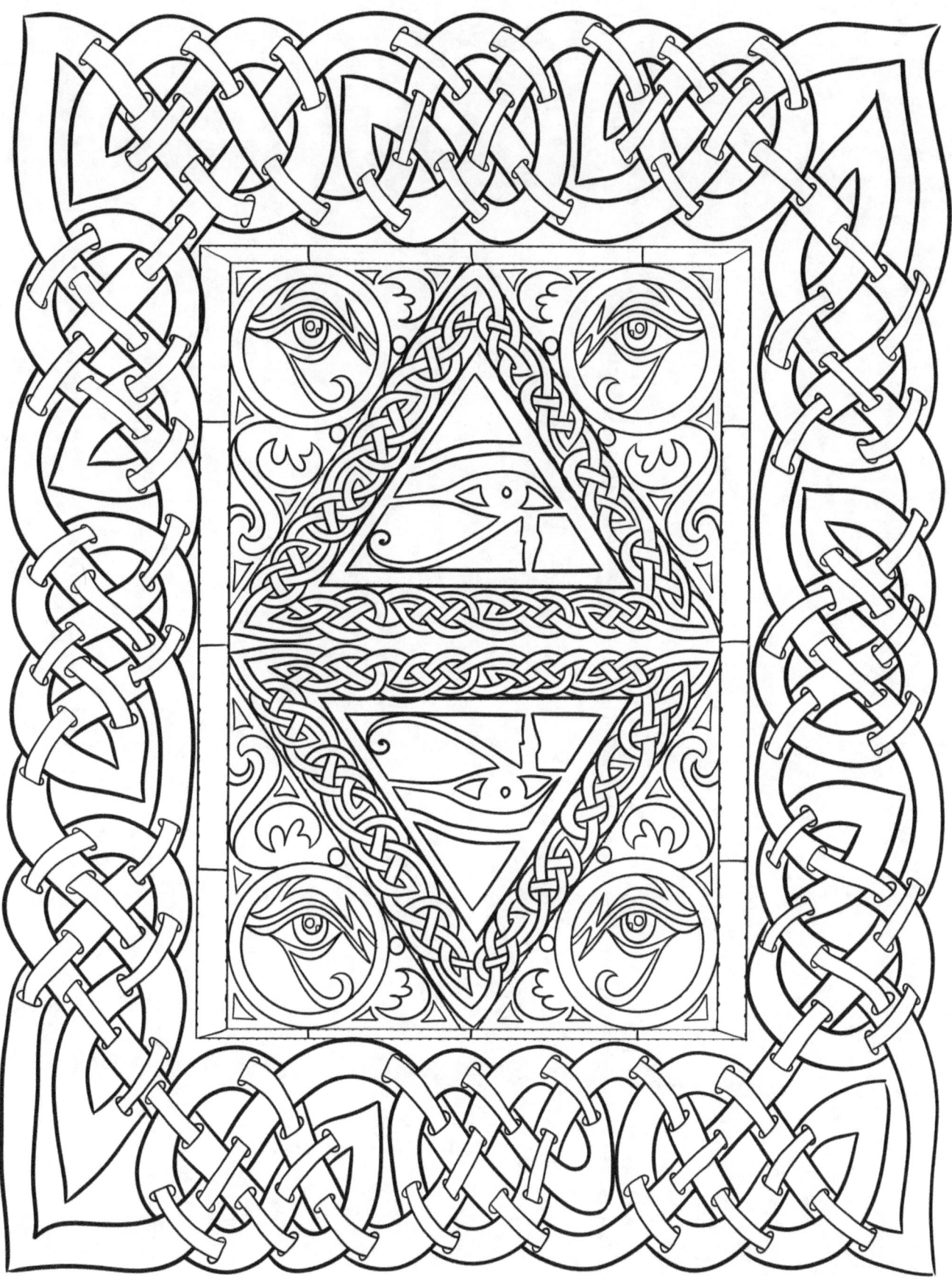

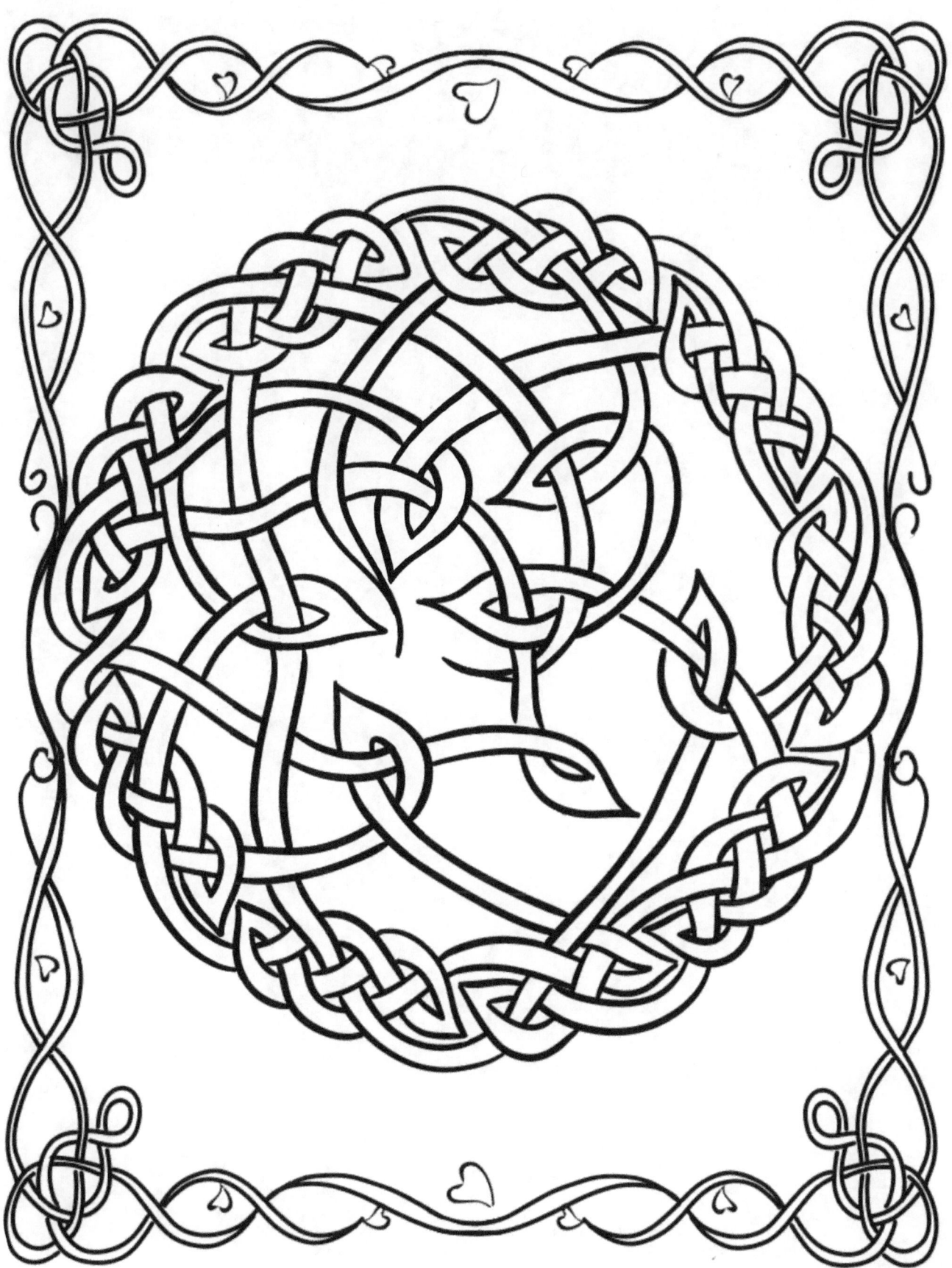

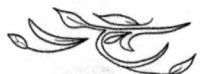

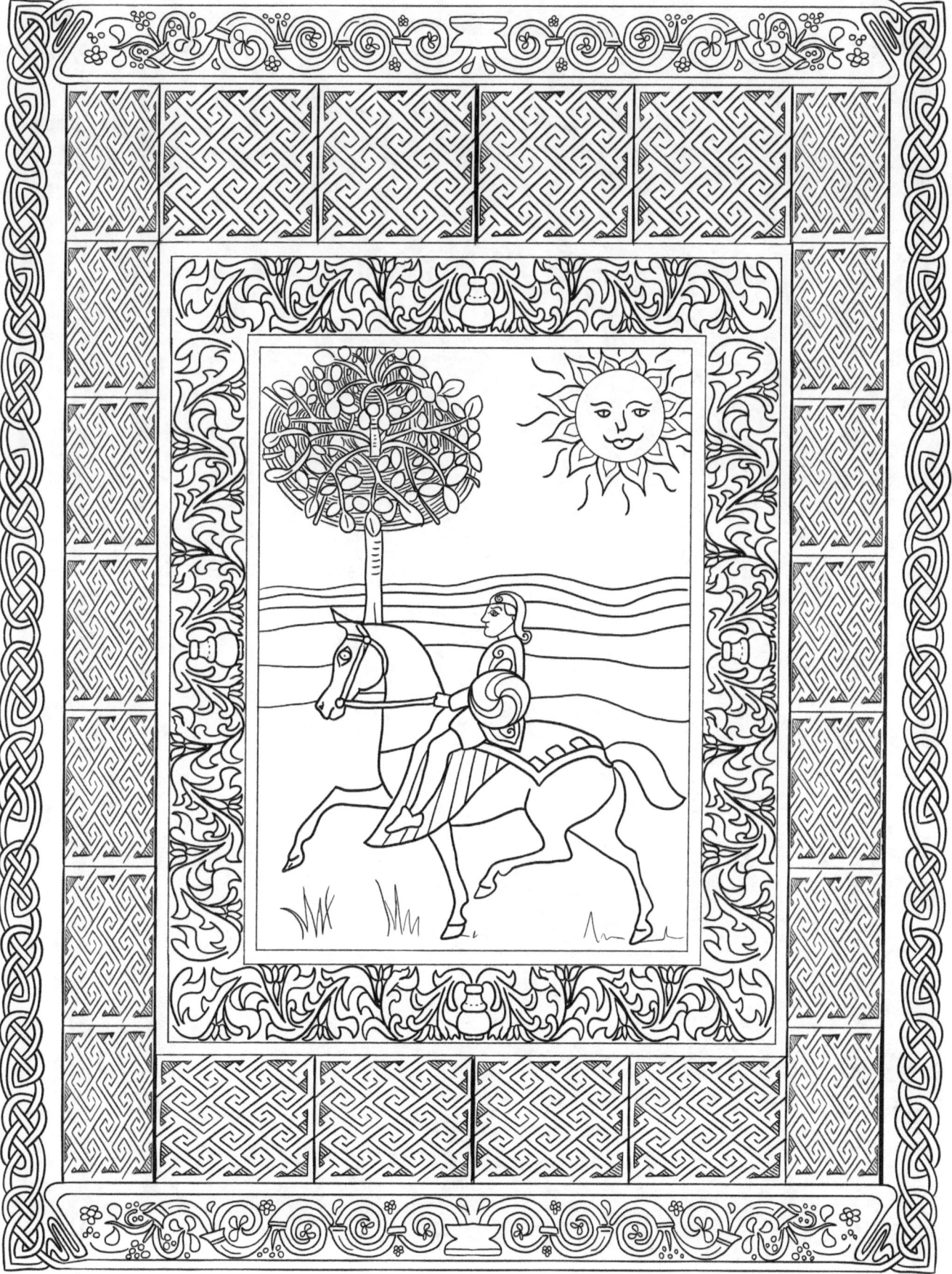

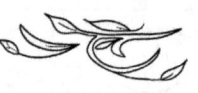

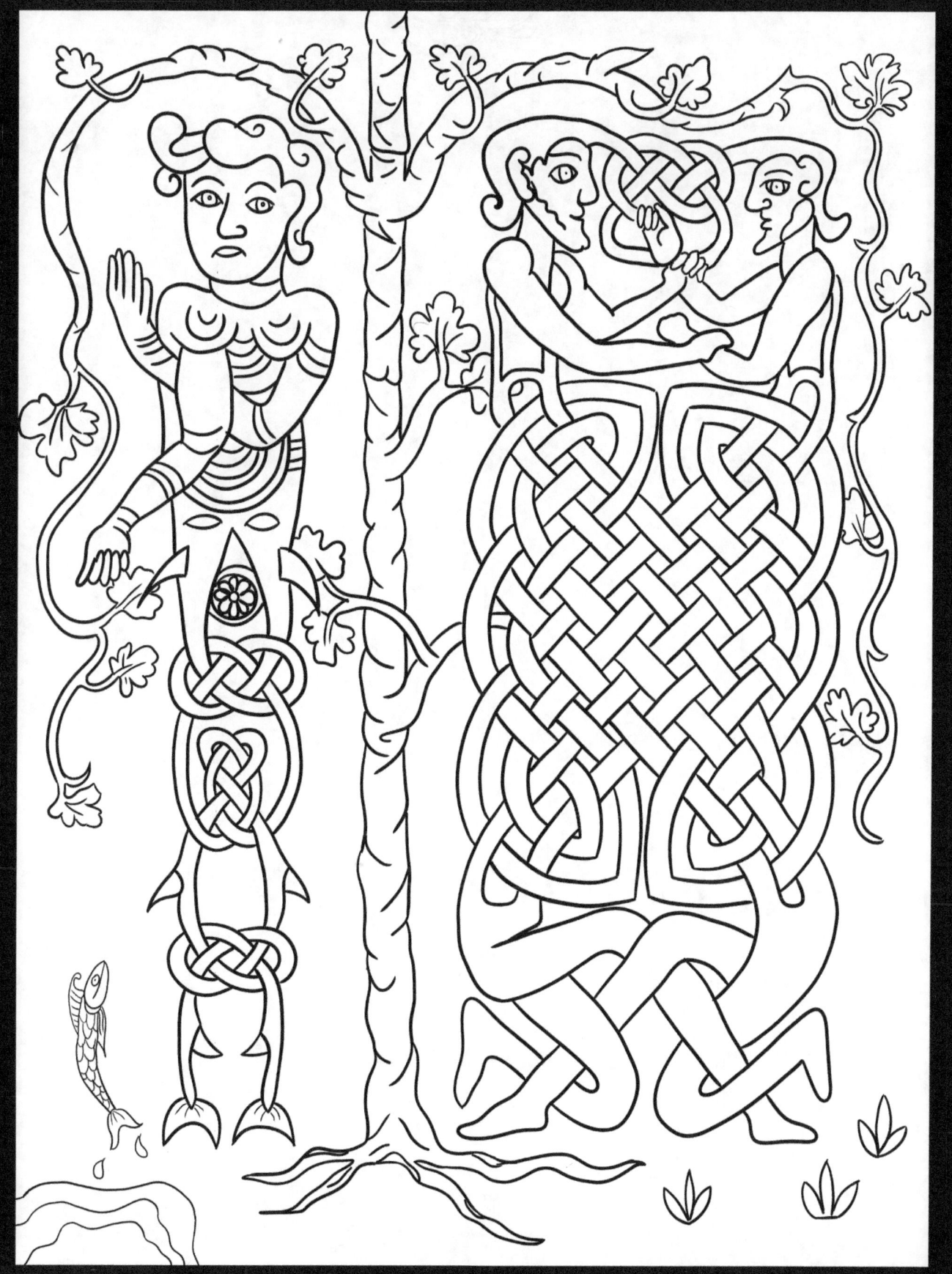

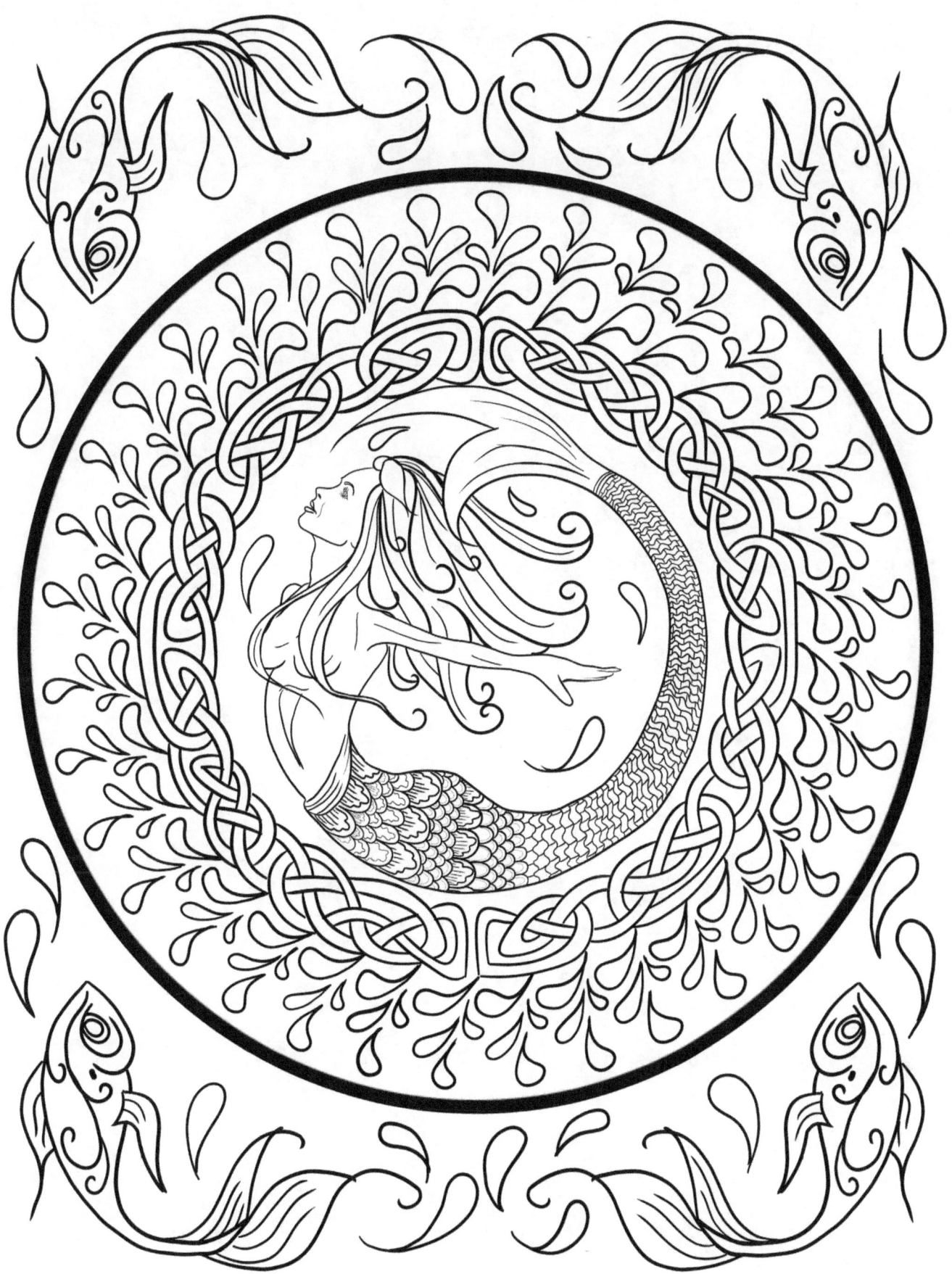

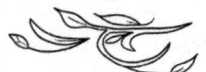

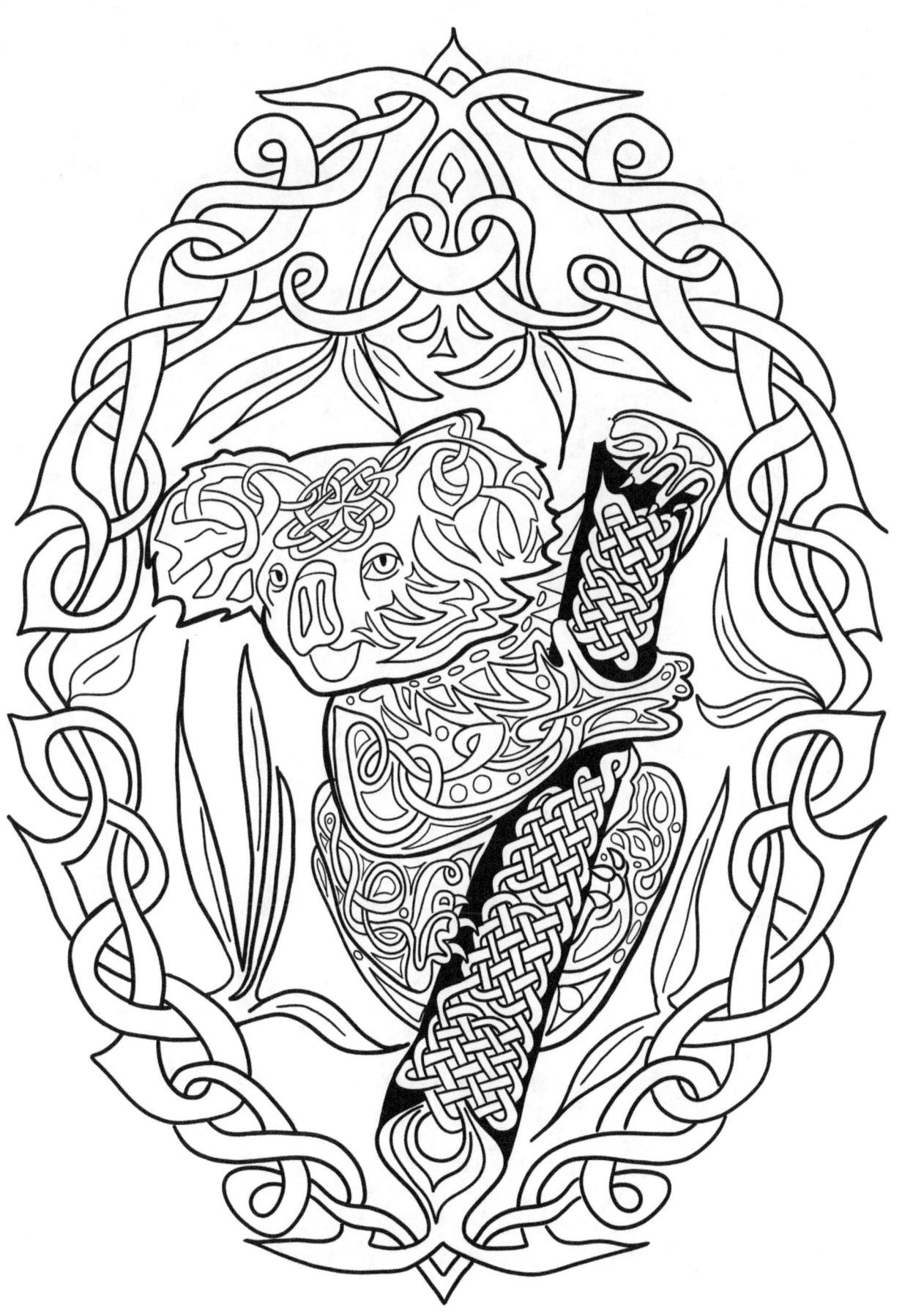

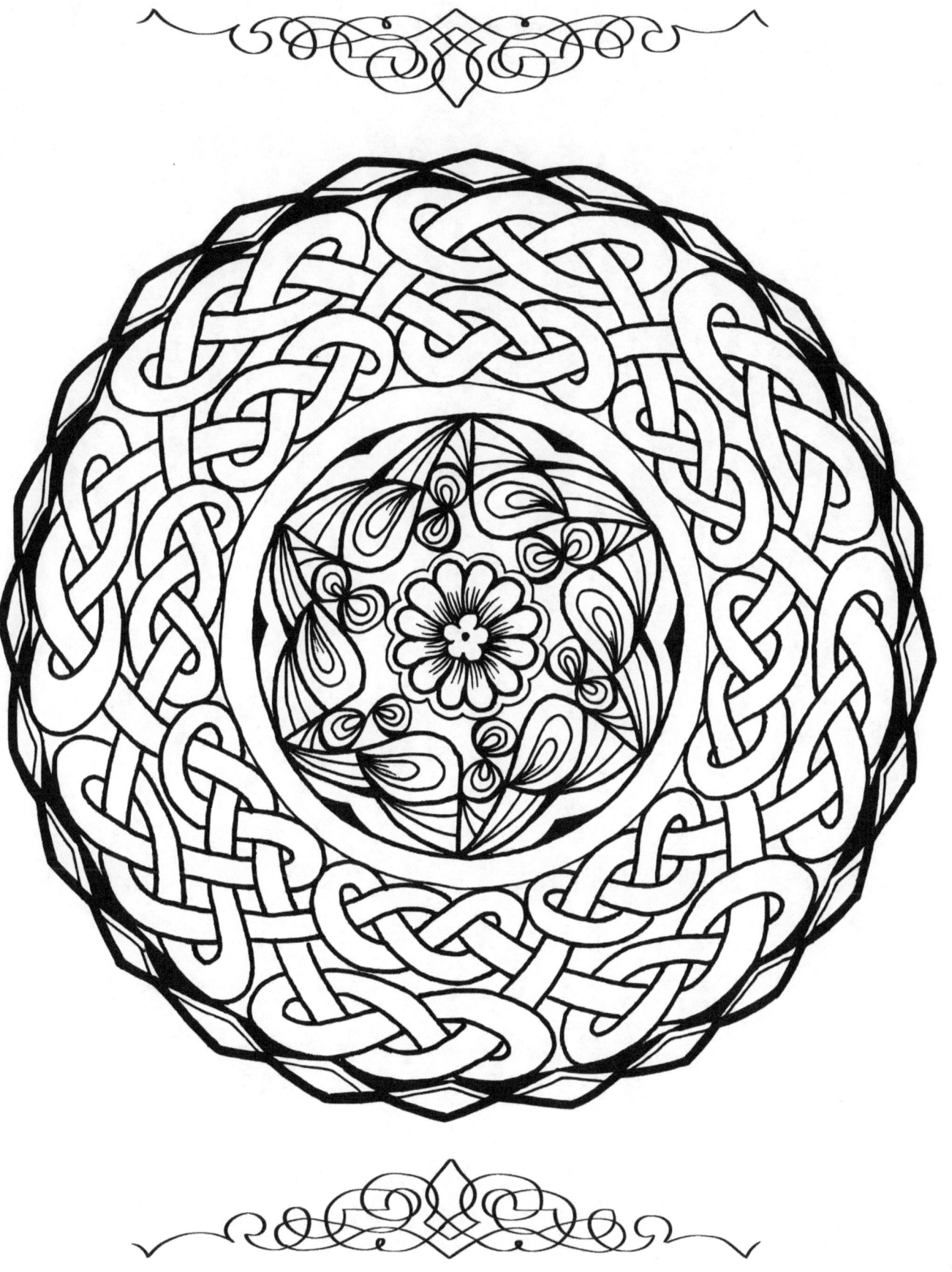

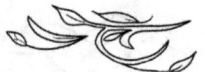

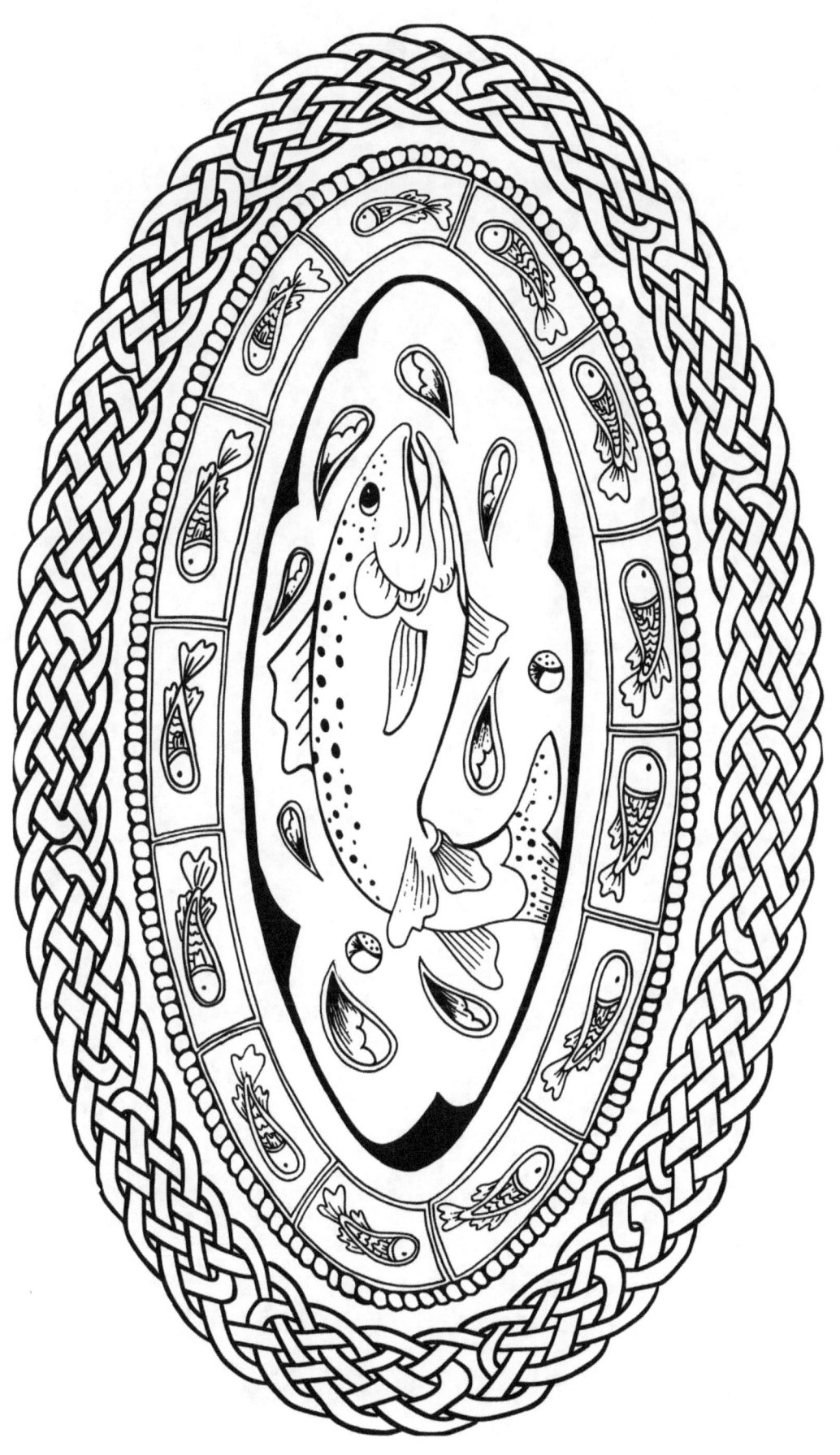

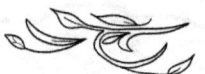

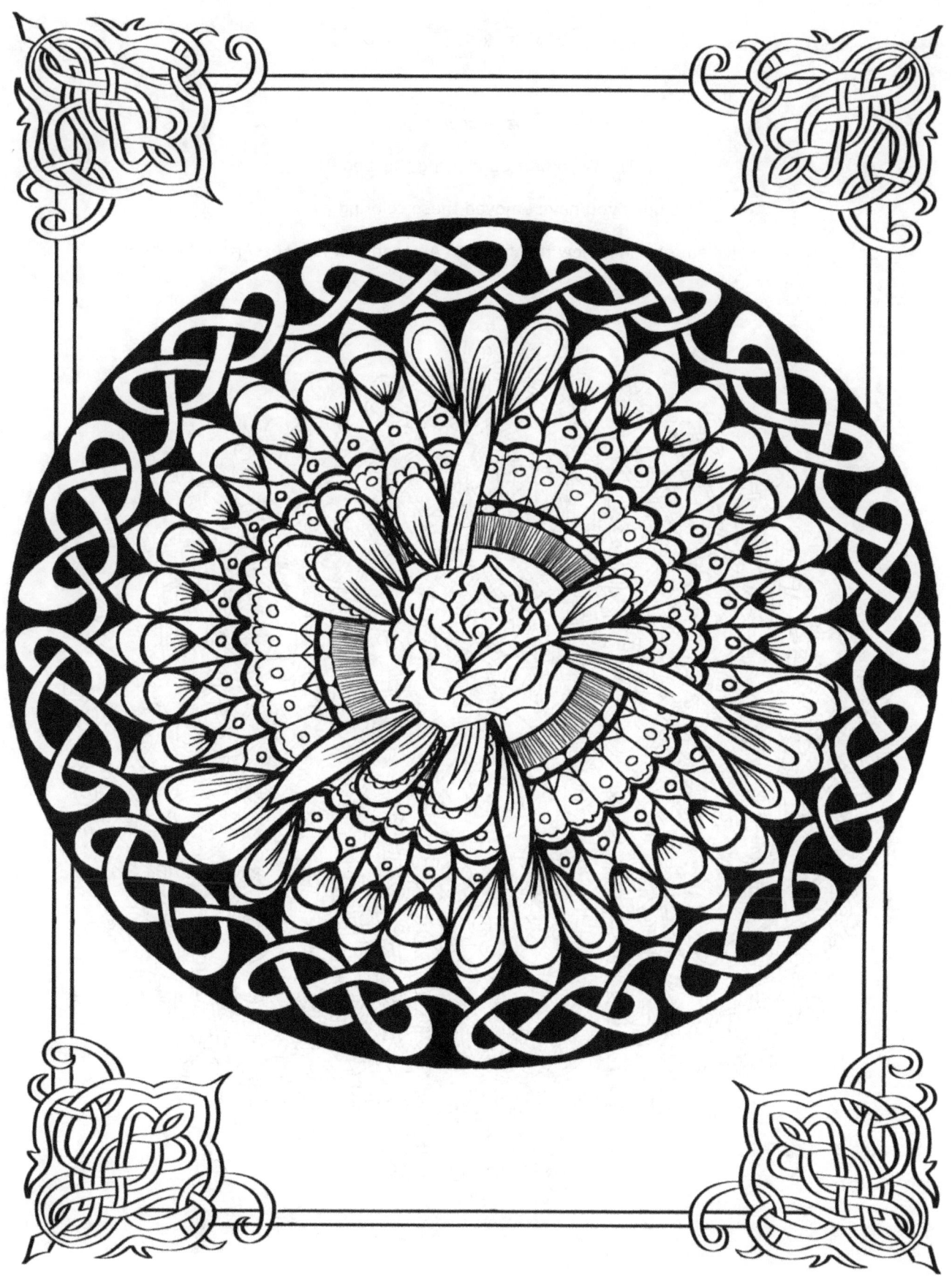

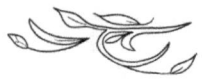

lozsart.com

Thank you for purchasing this book!

We hope you have enjoyed these coloring pages.

If you are satisfied, please review this book on Amazon and like LozsArt on facebook.

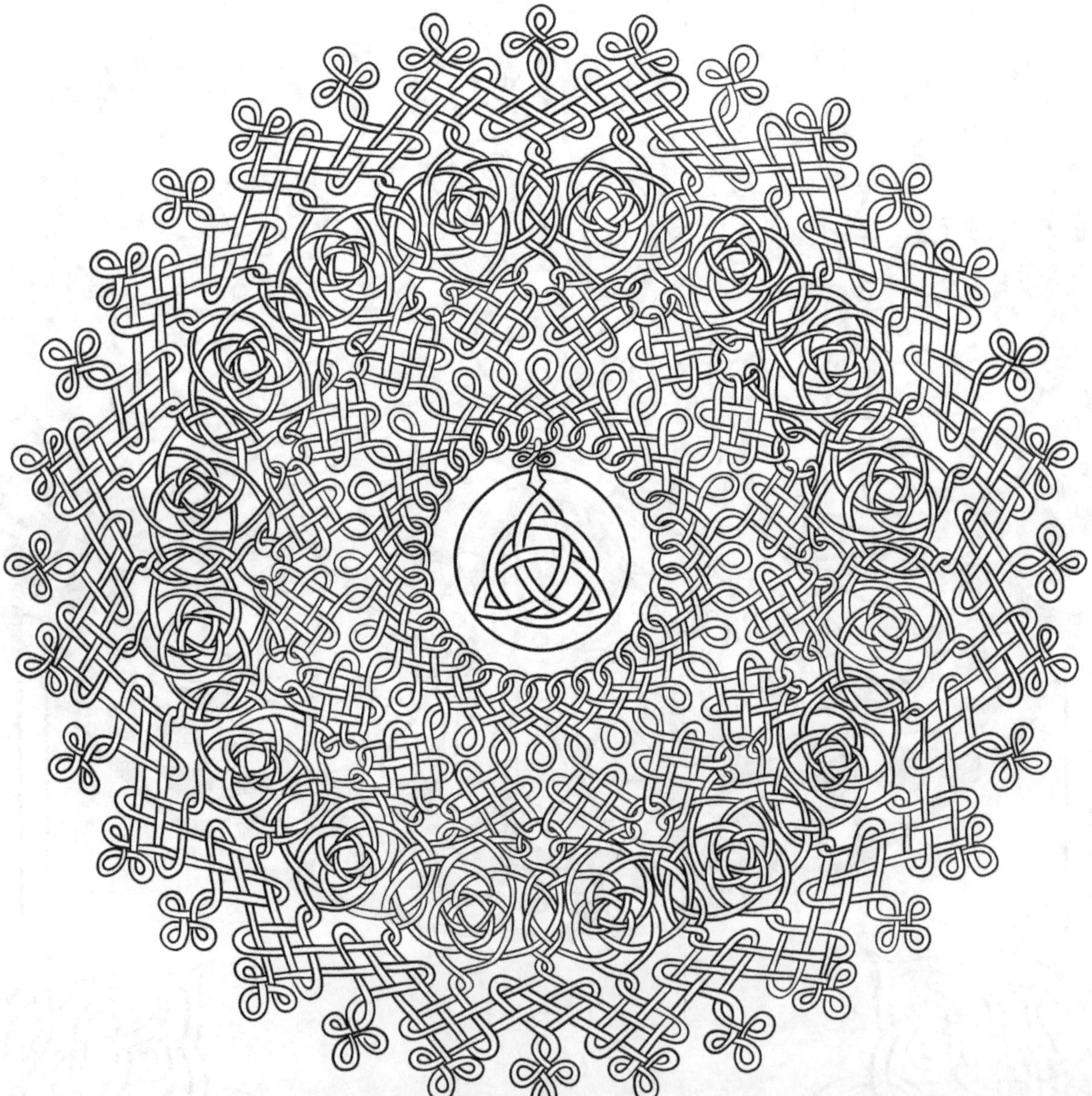

Leonard da Vinci's "Concatenation"

The End